DISTRIBUTION FOR THE SMALL BUSINESS

DISTRIBUTION FOR THE SMALL BUSINESS

Nicholas Mohr

KOGAN
PAGE

First published in Great Britain in 1990 by
Kogan Page Limited, 120 Pentonville Road,
London N1 9JN.

British Library Cataloguing in Publication Data
A CIP record for this book is available
from the British Library.

ISBN 0-7494-0081-1
ISBN 1-85091-462-1 Pbk

Typeset by DP Photosetting, Aylesbury
Printed and bound in Great Britain by
Biddles Limited, Guildford

Contents

Acknowledgements

The following organisations have kindly agreed to the publication of documents in the book:

Air Canada, Air waybill (page 83); Circle Freight International Ltd, Air waybill (page 84); Evergreen International (UK) Ltd, Bill of lading (pages 74-5); HM Customs and Excise, Single Administrative Document (page 87); IBM United Kingdom Ltd, EDI system (page 89); International Federation of Freight Forwarders Association (FIATA), Bill of lading (page 79); LEP Fairs and Exhibitions Ltd, ATA carnet (page 105); London Chamber of Commerce, Certificate of origin (page 68); MAT Transport Ltd, Certificate of shipment (page 86); Moonbridge Shippers Ltd, Bill of lading (page 80); Simplification of International Trade Procedures Board (SITPRO), Standard shipping note (page 71); Tate Telex and Continuous Stationery Ltd, International consignment note and dangerous goods note (page 102).

Preface

The attempt to distil almost 20 years' experience of transport into words is not an easy task. People within the transport industry, with few exceptions, are not known for their ability to write. It is an industry which depends on paper, but so much of it is incomprehensible!

The aim of this book is to provide a basic guide to transport for small businesses. Rather than becoming bogged down in technical details, such as how to complete Box 47 on a Single Administrative Document, I have tried to provide readers with a practical guide. I trust that by the end of the book you will know, for example, which basic documents are required for exports and imports. There are plenty of professional firms who are quite capable of filling them in on your behalf, but you should know what function they perform and roughly what they look like.

The book has been some time in gestation and could not have been written without the thorough grounding I received in transport for two years from Ritschard SA, Geneva, and subsequently for 12 years with the MAT Group in London. Much of what I was taught by these two leading international freight forwarders appears in this book.

In addition, I have relied on a panel of experts who have been kind enough to check the text and suggest alterations. In no order of priority, my thanks go to Steve Chapman, Bob Cross, Terry M King and Gordon Taylor. Their help has been invaluable, although the responsibility for any errors is mine alone. I am also grateful to the numerous organisations which have allowed me to reproduce their documents in the book. A full list appears in the Acknowledgements.

I have been given magnificent word processing and moral support by Marlene Turtle, and my editor at Kogan Page has shown patience beyond the call of duty. Finally, my thanks go to Sara Gilbert, author and wife 'extraordinaire', who has spent so much time translating my muddled English into words which can be published.

Nicholas Mohr
December 1989

Chapter 1

The Transport Decision

Transport is now front page news. Every newspaper carries regular reports about the crumbling infrastructure of the UK transport system. Regular users of British Rail suffer delays, overcrowding and inconvenience. Motorists face delays and frustration. Even taking a holiday has become a major headache with most holiday-makers forced to spend hours waiting for their aircraft to depart to the sun.

The inconvenience of commuting and travelling has forced UK transport on to the political agenda just because the inadequacies of the transport system affect most people every day. Now that the subject of transport has become important, politicians have come up with all sorts of different solutions to what is an immensely complex problem. Most people believe that more investment is required, but opinion is divided as to the proportion which should be dedicated to road and the proportion to rail. In addition, local lobbies are very powerful in determining where new rail or road links can be sited.

Small businesses are affected by the problems of organising an effective distribution strategy. A recent study, published by the Confederation of British Industry (CBI), estimated that traffic congestion was costing British businesses £1.5 billion per year. These additional costs can be quantified in many ways, but mainly relate to the delays suffered by vehicles on their daily journeys. Gradually, the number of deliveries any one vehicle can complete in a day falls, so the haulage firm is obliged to buy additional vehicles in order to maintain its service levels. Similarly, small businesses have to hold greater levels of stock if they cannot rely on receiving components and materials on a regular basis.

These problems extend to international distribution and more and more companies are involved in exporting and importing. In theory, sending goods to Paris should be as easy as sending them to Birmingham. Yet 'Europe' is still regarded by many small businesses as another planet – referring to the Continent as Europe is a fundamental error of perception which is unfortunately repeated far too often. The UK has always been a part of Europe, and those countries on the other side of the Channel are 'on the Continent' or 'on the mainland'.

Trading with the Continent does not have to be a logistical nightmare.

Mistakes are, however, often made, particularly by small firms who have not bothered to find out about the details of sending goods abroad. The result is normally a vehicle and goods which are blocked at foreign customs for two or three days until the correct documentation is available. With a little preparation the whole shipment could have moved smoothly to the customer.

Other small firms will focus their efforts on more distant markets and begin to handle export or import business with North America, the Far East or any other part of the world. The transport options for the more distant destinations are countless. Goods can be moved by sea, by air or by sea/air and can be packed into all types of different containers or shipped loose.

The first section of the book looks at the methods of physical distribution available. An examination of domestic distribution is followed by a look at methods of transport which are available within Europe. Air freight is growing rapidly, by about 8 per cent in volume terms per year, and it has an ever widening appeal for small firms. Sea transport, although slower, is still far more important as a method of transport and is described in some detail.

As important as the physical movement of the cargo is the documentation without which goods will at some stage be stopped. This applies equally to export and import shipments, and the main documents used are listed with examples provided.

Some types of goods require special handling and governments and international organisations issue detailed instructions intended to simplify procedures and protect all the parties involved. Chemicals require special arrangements as do exhibition goods, and the procedures for some of these more common special despatches are described.

Exporters and importers can decide or negotiate about the terms of sale which will apply to their traffic. There are many options to choose from as well as a great deal of confusion surrounding the subject.

Yet, even before the goods are shipped, thought must be given to the type of packing which is required. This cannot be considered in isolation – the choice of packing will influence the method of transport, or rather the method of transport will influence the type of packing. Insurance is another vital element – if the goods are lost or damaged, many a small business will face grave financial embarrassment. This does not prevent many firms from ignoring the potential danger and sending their goods off uninsured. The choice of transport should also be an integral part of a company's marketing strategy. Overseas buyers may re-order more frequently if goods arrive on schedule and in good condition.

The organisation of transport is, therefore, a vital decision for every business. The importance of transport is now more widely accepted by larger firms but the message has to spread to businesses of all sizes. Small businesses need to study their requirements and develop a distribution strategy which should cover both UK and overseas business. The strategy should not be a weighty document which is ignored from the moment it is printed. There is no need to put anything in writing! Rather, every firm should look at how transport, like cash flow, production or sales, is a vital part of the business. The companies ready to help small businesses to develop a distribution strategy are the freight forwarders, and Chapter 11 looks at how they operate and how to find a competent forwarder.

Transport affects the whole firm and its importance in terms of the company's resources devoted to transport will increase in the future. This is the concept behind the transport decisions which every small business has to make regularly. Serious readers can apply Chapter 12 on distribution, marketing and cash flow to their own company.

Finally, distribution patterns will have to change with the creation of the Single European Market, the opening of the Channel Tunnel and changes in data processing. A forecast of the likely effect of these developments is not attempted, but small businesses should be aware of the potential opportunities now. Transport has to move up the agenda for every small firm. This book will, I hope, provide a framework for taking the necessary transport decisions.

Chapter 2

Domestic Transport

Introduction

Every business has at some time to arrange for the delivery of goods to another part of the country. Some firms may have to deliver the occasional small package, while other companies despatch goods around the country every day. About 98 per cent of goods traffic in the UK moves by road. Other methods of domestic transport such as air or rail are, therefore, of little concern to most small businesses.

Although small firms are almost certain to use road transport, there are many different ways of organising domestic distribution by road. In addition, small businesses in particular should not neglect the option of sending goods by post.

Own account

The fundamental decision for any small business is whether to operate a vehicle and organise its own distribution. Companies which operate their own vehicles to carry their products are referred to as 'own account operators'. General haulage companies are called 'hire and reward operators' – these are companies which carry goods on behalf of other firms.

The decision whether to buy a vehicle depends on the particular circumstances of every firm. Many companies operate one vehicle which can handle local deliveries and collections, and all other work is handed over to independent hauliers. The requirements of one large customer may be sufficient reason to invest in a vehicle.

Having taken the decision to invest, the company is faced with choosing the type and model of vehicle and the method of finance. There are several trade publications (Appendix 2) which contain the latest information on commercial vehicle specifications and prices.

Vehicles can be purchased outright and for a company which needs only a small vehicle this is the easiest solution. There are other methods of purchase which have all types of advantages and disadvantages, including vehicle leasing or vehicle rental. A decision has to be taken in the light of the company's financial resources and the potential tax benefits or penalties.

For most small companies the advice must be to try to avoid buying a vehicle, even a small one, if this is at all possible. The main reason for this recommendation comes from an old management dictum 'Stick to the knitting'. This theory states that a manufacturer of, for example, pillowcases knows how to produce and market pillowcases as this is his core business. No one has told him how to run a distribution operation but there are many specialised firms who have the necessary expertise. Running a vehicle is not simply a question of instructing a driver where to go each day. The vehicle needs to be licensed and maintained and there may even be tachograph regulations to worry about if it has a gross weight of over 3.5 tonnes.

The other major consideration against operating one's own vehicles is cost. Like any other capital investment, a road vehicle must be on the move continuously if it is to pay its way. The greater the distance the vehicle travels, the lower the cost per mile of ownership. Therefore, it is uneconomical to own a vehicle which may be working only on three days out of five. Large hauliers ensure that their lorries are on the road for at least six days a week.

Most companies are surprised by the real costs of running a vehicle once such items as drivers' wages, depreciation, road tax and maintenance are added up. *Motor Transport*, a trade paper which circulates widely in the transport industry, publishes cost tables three or four times a year. These tables give full details of all the costs involved in running vehicles of different sizes as well as the cost per mile. In the October 1989 edition, the estimated cost of running a small diesel van with a one-tonne payload was £1.34 per mile based on 10,000 miles per year or £0.63 per mile based on 25,000 miles. Larger vehicles are much more expensive to operate. For the more ambitious company which contemplates buying a large 12 metre trailer and tractor (Chapter 3), the operating costs are even more daunting – £1.75 per mile based on 30,000 miles per year and £1.05 based on 70,000 miles. The conclusion from these figures is that, in general terms, vehicle purchase should be avoided, particularly by small businesses. The alternative to operating one's own vehicle is contract distribution which is covered on pages 23–24.

Express services

One of the most widely used words in transport is express – every type of transport seems to have the express tag. The trend has led to a great deal of confusion as express services are poorly defined. For some companies an express service means delivery on the same day, for others it means delivery within 24 hours; indeed, express can cover goods which are delivered within two or three days. So the first thing to discover about an express service is the company's definition of express. There are, however, broad categories of services which can be outlined.

Motor-cycle messengers and minicabs

The most visible couriers are the motor-cycle messengers who risk life and limb as they weave through the traffic in all the major cities. Their service is normally quick but a motor-cycle is not designed to carry large amounts of freight. In practical terms, consignments handed over to motor-cycle services must be small and light, so most of the goods carried consist of documents, contracts and samples.

Most of the messengers are self-employed and own their own motor bikes. This means that setting up such a business is very easy – it requires only a telephone and a couple of willing messengers who are paid according to the mileage covered. This system also results in many firms setting up in business and closing down a short time later. Few companies operating in this sector of the market have established reputations and care must be taken before entrusting a valuable document or contract to them. There is a trade body which represents the sector – the Despatch Association – but it maintains a low profile and is quite incapable of policing malpractice. There is no common accepted code of practice among the membership of the Despatch Association so even the trade body is of no real assistance to potential users.

An alternative to a motor-cycle messenger is using a minicab or taxi. Most of these companies are happy to deliver small packages or documents, although most firms limit coverage to their local area. Many minicab firms are linked to motor-cycle messenger services.

Courier and small parcel services

Courier and small parcel services have a better pedigree than motor-cycle messengers and there are some well-established companies in this sector of the market, including Securicor and TNT. A courier and small parcel service tends to operate with a small van so it can collect larger consignments than can be transported on a motor-cycle. Yet even with a small van, the weight limitations on consignments are quite low, although each company sets its own restrictions. All the services are door to door.

Some courier companies limit their operations within a local area while others provide national coverage. Within the city centres, small vans are used because they are more manoeuvrable. The larger companies have depots on the outskirts of the major cities, and all the goods are brought to the depot for sorting before they are re-despatched, often to a central depot, referred to as a hub. Many of these hubs are located in the Midlands and only a short distance from a motorway junction. They spring to life when vehicles arrive from the outlying depots and unload thousands of consignments for sorting and re-forwarding. The major part of this operation occurs at night; the following day the goods are delivered from the local depot to the consignee.

The parcels companies have invested enormous sums in depot networks, data processing systems and vehicles, and delivery within a day does not allow any room for error. One of the major (and insoluble) problems now facing the parcels operators is traffic congestion, particularly in South East England and on the overburdened motorways. Many of these companies have been forced to revise their operational procedures in recent years to take account of the inevitable delays. When a vehicle fails to turn up or is delayed collecting or delivering an important consignment, it is easy to blame the transport operator; but usually the vehicle is immobilised in a traffic jam somewhere. This kind of problem is now an unfortunate fact of commercial life. It is, therefore, important to have some sympathy for the frustrations and problems which now face every transport company because of the widespread congestion throughout the country. This does not excuse sloppy performance but not every error can be laid at the door of the transporter.

In some ways small companies can help their suppliers and also streamline their own distribution operation. Many firms insist on asking for collections and deliveries to take place at a precise time. Sometimes this cannot be avoided, but in most instances it is far better to give the transport operator more latitude. Instead of insisting on a collection at 11am, ask the company to call in during the morning. Lunchtime presents another problem for drivers who are most upset when they have struggled through a traffic jam, only to discover that the firm is closed for an hour. If possible, leave someone on duty during lunch to avoid further delay. Traffic congestion has forced many transport firms to start work extremely early – vehicles are on the road from 5am – so the possibility of arranging an early collection or delivery is usually welcome. If a vehicle can call at 6am, it will always be on time – a further advantage.

The courier companies will provide one-, two- or three-day delivery services. There are same-day services available and, within a certain distance, a same-day delivery is not difficult to arrange. Over a longer distance, a same-day service is possible but expensive. The major deciding factor for a same day service is the distance and the existing transport links. There are companies which are capable of arranging a same-day service but it may be cheaper and more reliable to go yourself or to send an employee. A consignment which has to be delivered in another part of the country today is, by definition, extremely urgent, so it is worthwhile ensuring that there will be no mistakes before handing the consignment over to a carrier.

One-, two- or three-day services are now commonplace in the parcels industry. The services are usually given different names, such as Next Day, Standard and Economy, and the prices come down as the transit time increases. This is a perfectly logical method of charging, as delivering consignments is more expensive when the timetable is tight. Most of the courier and parcels carriers have brochures containing their tariffs which are usually easy to calculate. They also have sales representatives who will be pleased to call and explain the services to potential customers. As a further incentive, the carriers offer discounts for regular business. These discounts are based either on the number of consignments moved through their services or on turnover.

Royal Mail parcels

The largest domestic parcel carrier is still the Post Office which has now divided its activities between parcels and letters. The parcels division of the Royal Mail operates under the name Royal Mail Parcels (RMP). Probably every company uses RMP on some occasions, and RMP can be used from time to time or on a contract basis.

The great advantage of RMP is that they have a presence in every high street – a total of 3000 receiving offices throughout the UK. Parcels can be delivered during normal working hours to any main Post Office. RMP will also come and collect from business premises on a regular basis – daily or less frequently if required. There are normally certain volume commitments if RMP comes to collect – they do not want to send a van to collect just one or two parcels.

The weight limit for RMP domestic parcels is 25 kilos, and no one side of the parcel must exceed 1.5 metres in length. Larger shipments can be sent through RMP, as long as the goods can be divided up into several smaller parcels. There is a final stipulation that the length and width of the parcel must not exceed 3 metres in total. The cost of sending such a parcel anywhere in the UK from October 1989 is £5.50. The pricing policy of RMP does not change in accordance with distance, so this maximum charge covers the delivery of the parcel to a customer a few miles away as well as one situated on a remote Scottish island. This uniform price is the advantage and disadvantage of RMP – no one can serve the outlying areas as cheaply but local deliveries may be considered a little expensive.

Although RMP works to a published price list, companies with regular business can use special services targeted at small firms. There are three types of service available: Standard service, Super 24 and Super 48. The Standard service is aimed at companies which send a minimum of 1000 parcels per year and require a two- to three-day transit time. Super 24 and Super 48 are guaranteed 24- or 48-hour delivery services. The Super services provide full documentation, including proof of delivery and loss or damage insurance.

In recent years, RMP has made strenuous efforts to improve its image. But it still has a reputation for unreliability, and this was not helped by the postal strike which closed down the whole system for several weeks in September and October 1988. Under the normal RMP service, the parcel disappears into the system and there is no satisfactory way of knowing its whereabouts. If the service were totally reliable, this would not matter, but unfortunately no one can be quite certain how long it will take for a parcel to be delivered.

In order to keep track of its parcels traffic, RMP has introduced a tracking and tracing system which registers every parcel at the time of collection and at the time of delivery. Although this is an attempt to address the problem of monitoring traffic as it moves through the system, there is still no control of the parcels while they are in transit. RMP has tried hard to improve its service levels in recent years, but the organisation has still to improve its image with small businesses.

Datapost

The Datapost service of RMP is the premium service which does ensure delivery within the UK overnight. All parcels which are destined for main towns are delivered by 10am the following day, while those items for outlying areas are usually delivered before midday.

The weight limit for Datapost shipments is 30 kilos, and the dimensions are the same as for ordinary parcels (see page 20). As a premium service, Datapost is considerably more expensive than the ordinary parcel service. The minimum charge is £14 for any consignment up to 10 kilos, and the prices rise to a maximum of £26 for a 30 kilo parcel. The Datapost system is used widely – it was originally intended to serve companies who need to send urgent computer tapes around the country, but is now used by every type of business.

Some critics accuse RMP of making a virtue out of necessity by introducing the Datapost service. The argument runs that customers who want a reliable delivery must use Datapost, but RMP can only sell such a premium service because the regular service is unreliable. This may well be true but the situation, however unsatisfactory, has to be accepted. There is always the option of sending urgent goods via Datapost and less urgent goods through the normal parcels service. Whatever decision is taken, RMP deserves to be considered as a potential carrier of small parcels traffic.

General haulage traffic

Most express carriers and courier operators have a weight restriction, so larger consignments have to be handed over to haulage contractors who operate larger vehicles. This is the type of freight which moves up and down the motorway system every day and is carried by thousands of independent, competing haulage firms.

The UK haulage industry consists of a few large companies and thousands of smaller ones. The large companies include such well-known names as NFC, formerly the National Freight Corporation, and TDG, which stands for the Transport Development Group. They are divided up into specialist divisions which are defined by the products they carry. Both NFC and TDG have divisions which specialise in the carriage of chilled or frozen foods and clothes. The large companies are no longer so interested in 'spot business' which is left more to the smaller hauliers. 'Spot business' comes from firms who contact their hauliers whenever there is some cargo to move. There is no contractual arrangement between the customer and the haulier except when some goods are being transported. Although at first glance this may seem an unstable financial climate for a domestic haulier, most firms build up solid relationships with a number of customers. The exact volume and destination of freight will vary from day to day, but a working relationship is established and most hire and reward hauliers have regular business.

General haulage companies use all types of different vehicle – some are covered and some are uncovered. Uncovered vehicles are often referred to as flat vehicles, and the goods carried receive only limited protection from sheets which are pulled over and fastened to the superstructure of the trailer. Flat vehicles are easier to load and unload but the goods are much more susceptible to damage from water. This limits their use to strong robust goods which will be unharmed by limited exposure to the weather.

Covered vehicles have either solid sides in the same way as a small van or a thick tarpaulin which extends over the whole length of the lorry. These types of vehicle are much more suitable for more delicate cargo. There are hundreds of models which hauliers can buy and, from the customer's point of view, the exact choice of vehicle is not important as long as it is appropriate for the job in hand.

General haulage contractors have a trade association – the Road Haulage Association (RHA). The majority of reputable hauliers belong to the RHA and display their membership by including the small RHA insignia on their letterhead. Membership of the RHA means that the haulier will operate under the RHA Conditions of Carriage. These define the relationship between the carrier and the trader, and the conditions become important when something goes wrong. Under the RHA conditions, the haulier is liable up to a maximum sum of £800 per tonne in respect of loss or misdelivery. There are all sorts of other conditions which have to be met before a haulier will accept liability and settle a claim, but the £800 figure is quite insufficient compensation for most categories of cargo.

The solution to this problem is for the small customer to take out transit insurance (Chapter 10) either directly through an insurance broker or through the carrier. Yet, even with the perceived weaknesses of the RHA conditions, it is far better to place business through a member of the RHA than with a company not in the association. Membership of the RHA does mean a certain degree of professional probity, although financial stability is not guaranteed by membership! Companies which are not members of the RHA often operate under far more restrictive terms than the RHA conditions, and this is another reason for using a member of the RHA.

General hauliers will normally quote freight rates on a per tonne basis with a minimum charge. If a small company has 3 tonnes to move from London to Glasgow, and the rate is £20 per tonne, the cost is £60. The weight/volume ratio is 80 cubic feet per tonne, so goods which have dimensions in excess of 80 cubic feet per tonne are charged on their volume not on the weight. In the same example, if the goods weighed 3 tonnes but had dimensions of 480 cubic feet, this represents 6 tonnes, so the cost is £120. The endearing commitment of the road haulage industry to cubic feet rather than cubic metres (the metric system) causes a great deal of confusion not least among companies who use domestic hauliers for the first part of the journey overseas. Freight forwarders use different weight/volume ratios for road, sea and air transport but they are at least based on the metric system. Exporters and importers have to be adept at using one conversion factor for domestic transport and another for international movement. It is simpler perhaps to give the haulier the weight and dimensions of the consignment in question and he will provide an all-inclusive price.

Contract distribution

One of the fastest growing areas of domestic transport is contract distribution. It is not widely known that most of the large retailers, such as Marks & Spencer, Sainsbury and Tesco, do not organise their own distribution. The goods are transported from factories and depots to the stores by haulage contractors who work under long-term contract. The vehicles are painted in the livery of the customer but they belong to and are operated by outside contractors.

Contract distribution is not, however, an option only for large companies. There are many medium-sized and small firms which have opted for contract distribution in recent years, and haulage firms are interested in smaller contracts which may be as little as one vehicle.

The basis of contract distribution is a commitment by both the company and the haulier. The arrangement is formalised by a contract which lasts usually for at least three years and often longer. In exchange for this contract, the haulier will invest in as many vehicles as are required and also have them painted in the client's livery. Drivers are allocated to the contract, and the vehicles are dedicated to working on behalf of the customer. The trader is not involved in maintenance or repair and, even in the event of a major breakdown, another vehicle will be allocated to the contract. In exchange for this level of service, the haulier is paid on a predetermined basis.

As an option, contract distribution is feasible only for small firms with a regular volume of goods to deliver every day. Companies without a regular flow of traffic should not consider it as they will end up paying for idle vehicles. Yet contract distribution companies are able to supply small vehicles under contract as well as large. A company which has 15 or 20 small consignments to deliver every day within a 50-mile radius may do well to look at the possibility of contract distribution. The haulier becomes an extension of the company and the business is spared all the problems involved in operating its own vehicle. There is also the further option of sharing a contract with another firm situated in the neighbourhood. Together, the companies might have sufficient business to justify signing a contract.

Rail

The use of rail for domestic distribution is not a viable option. Companies which use rail are large producers of bulk commodities such as coal, steel or chemicals. British Rail (BR) has no real service to offer small shippers with the exception of Red Star.

Red Star parcels
BR is involved with the parcels market through its Red Star service. This is based on the railway network, and Red Star depots are located at all the main stations including the London termini. Red Star is primarily a station-to-station service whereby BR sends goods on Intercity trains or on dedicated parcels trains. In most cases, goods are delivered to the station, and the consignee will arrange to collect the consignment from the arrival station. There is also the option of a door-to-door service using Red Star – deliveries can be arranged before 9.30am, 10.30am or 12.30pm to virtually any destination in the UK. The three delivery schedules attract a reducing level of surcharge.

Red Star is an extremely quick service, particularly when goods are moving between two well-served railway stations. For example, a shipment which is handed in at Manchester Piccadilly in the morning will normally be available for collection at Euston station, London in the early part of the afternoon. Red Star can offer that elusive same day service discussed earlier in the chapter.

The weight limit for a single Red Star package is 100 kilos, and the maximum permitted dimensions of one package are 100cm (length), 50cm (breadth) and 50cm (height). Most of the traffic on Red Star services is much smaller than this; there are no sophisticated handling facilities at the

Summary of main parcel services in the UK

Method	Speed of delivery	Weight/size limitations	Door to door	Cost
Motor-cycles, minicabs, taxicabs	Same day	Variable	✓ Mainly local	Local charges apply
Couriers and small parcel services	Overnight 1 day 2 days 3 days	Variable	✓	Varies according to distance and speed of delivery
Royal Mail Parcels	24 hours 48 hours 2–3 days	Maximum 25 kg; total length and width 3 metres	✓	Countrywide uniform rates, reducing with slower delivery
Datapost	Overnight, morning delivery	Maximum 30kg	✓	Minimum charge up to 10kg
Red Star (British Rail)	Same day Next day	Maximum 100 kg; size 100 × 50 × 50cm	✓ or station to station	Varies according to distance and time of day
Own vehicle	You decide	You decide	✓	Overheads plus running costs
Contract service	As contract	As contract	✓	Contract price agreed over fixed period

stations so most of the traffic consists of urgent documents, small packages and samples.

Documentation

Documentation for domestic transport is easy. There are no legal requirements except in the case of hazardous goods. Most hauliers will insist on completing a collection or delivery note which provides details of the collection and delivery points and a brief description of the goods.

It is customary for the sender of the goods to ask the driver to sign a collection note when picking up the goods. The first note confirms the number of packages and that the goods are in good condition at the time of collection. The main point of the delivery note is to obtain a signature from the consignee when the goods are delivered as it confirms the safe arrival of the consignment. If there is a discrepancy, it is always advisable to note it down on the delivery note or to add the word 'unchecked' to the signature. In most cases, the consignee has three days to notify the haulier of any loss or damage to the consignment, and this must be confirmed in writing within seven days. In these circumstances, it is always safer to inspect the goods soon after their arrival rather than wait for several days to open the packages. Any claim after a delay will be far harder to press.

The consignor may provide the driver with invoices and a packing list. Unlike exports or imports, there are no customs checks on internal traffic so there is no real need for these documents.

Chapter 3

Transport Within Europe

Introduction

Businesses of all sizes are involved in transporting goods to and from other parts of Europe. Even before the UK became a member of the European Community (EC), trade with its future partners had been growing rapidly and this trend has continued to the present day.

The mainland of Europe is the UK's most important export market, and traders are more likely to buy or sell goods there than in any other part of the world. Groups of countries within Europe include Scandinavia and the Benelux countries (Belgium, the Netherlands and Luxembourg).

Of particular importance are the trading blocks which now dominate Europe. The largest is the European Community and the next is the European Free Trade Association (EFTA).

Members of the European Community (EC)

Belgium	Luxembourg
Denmark	Netherlands
France	Italy
Germany	Portugal
Greece	Spain
Irish Republic	United Kingdom

Members of the European Free Trade Association (EFTA)

Austria	Norway
Finland	Sweden
Iceland	Switzerland

Most small companies are unlikely to become involved in organising shipments to or from Eastern Europe. The buyers and sellers there normally organise their own transport in order to preserve foreign exchange and use national transport companies.

All modes of transport are used to move cargo between the UK and other parts of Europe – air, container, rail and road. The dominant method of transport is the road trailer, which has increased in popularity since the advent of the Roll-on/Roll-off (Ro-Ro) ferry.

Air freight

Within Europe air freight has lost many of its attractions in recent years, yet air freight cannot be discounted entirely, particularly for the more distant countries.

The development of express road carriers has resulted in a loss by airlines of a great deal of traffic. The loss has been particularly severe over the shorter distances – to Belgium, the Ruhr area of Germany, Luxembourg, Northern France and the Netherlands. Road operators guarantee anything from a 24- to a 72-hour service to these destinations. This is often a great deal more reliable than air freight. Although the airport-to-airport transit time is rapid, shippers are more interested in the door-to-door transit time, and road operators can achieve a similar or faster door-to-door transit time than airlines.

The other problem facing the airlines on short-haul routes is that turn-round times at the airports have been severely reduced to maximise flying time. This limits the opportunities for carrying freight on the aircraft and, therefore, many airlines now despatch goods to the closer destinations by road. This is common practice and, while a shipper may be under the impression that the goods are going to Paris by air, it is possible that they are moving across to France by a road vehicle under contract to the airline.

For normal overnight or two-day delivery services, the choice is between air freight or road, and in most instances the goods will in any case travel by road. For the more distant countries within Europe, such as Finland, Greece, Italy or Spain, air freight is still quicker. Remember, however, that a road trailer will travel from the UK to northern Italy or northern Spain within two to three days, and it is not uncommon for air freight to take a similar time from door to door.

In recent years, however, the airlines have tried to recapture some of the traffic lost to trailer operators. Having previously concentrated most of their marketing resources on long-haul routes, the airlines are now making efforts to win back short-haul cargo. The efforts will become more pronounced as the new generation of short-haul, wide-body Boeing 767s come into service from 1990. These new jets, to be used extensively for intra-European air traffic, have a larger and more accessible freight capacity than existing aircraft. This will undoubtedly act as an incentive to the airlines to try to attract more freight.

While air freight cannot normally be recommended for shorter journeys, emergency shipments should be sent by air. This is the only way of ensuring a same-day delivery to, for example, Paris or Frankfurt. Special arrangements to handle such a shipment will have to be made with a freight forwarder as many passenger flights do not accept freight.

Another factor influencing the choice between air freight and road is the distance from the consignor and consignee to the relevant airports. If there are no regular flights from the nearest airport, this factor will militate in favour of road. If, however, a major airport with direct connections is easily accessible, air freight may be the preferred choice.

Some of the European airlines now market a door-to-door delivery service which means that they will collect the consignment, arrange all the documentation, despatch the goods and deliver them to the customer overseas in accordance with a predetermined timetable.

Although still relatively new, these services from the airlines can be expected to develop over the next few years. The airlines also offer a daily on-board courier facility linking the UK with most other commercial centres in Europe. The courier accompanies the goods and this helps to speed up customs formalities. After neglecting intra-European freight for many years, the airlines now offer a range of services which will certainly provide them with more business in the future.

Express operators

One group of companies which uses air extensively within Europe is the express operators. These companies, which include such names as DHL, Federal Express, TNT-Ipec, UPS and XP Express, have grown extremely rapidly in recent years. Most of these companies are Australian or American owned and they have a high public profile. The express operators offer a door-to-door service at an all-inclusive price with a variety of transit times – normally 24, 48 or 72 hours. To provide these rapid guaranteed transit times, they use a combination of road vehicles and aircraft.

The road vehicles collect and deliver the consignments from large hubs and aircraft fly every night between the hubs. Many of the express companies organise their operations on a hub and spoke system. This image comes from the wheel of a bicycle which has a central hub and spokes which link into the hub. For an express operator, the hub is the central depot. Every consignment is first collected by a local depot, and once a day all the shipments are transferred to the central hub. Here, after sorting, the vehicles return to their local areas with the goods destined for their depot. Many of the hubs are highly sophisticated computer-controlled sorting centres, handling tens of thousands of small packages every day.

The freight-only aircraft are either owned or leased by the express operators; they comply with modern noise level regulations so that night-time flying is permitted. These aircraft also fly between smaller airports which attach a great importance to freight and are located near major commercial and industrial centres. In the UK, the express operators make extensive use of Birmingham, East Midlands, Luton and Southend airports. On the Continent, several operators are based in Brussels (Belgium) while others use Cologne/Bonn in West Germany.

Because consignments are travelling by air, the express operators limit the size of any one individual package but not the size of the total consignment. Every operator has a different limit depending on the size of aircraft, but in practical terms every package should be capable of being manhandled. The express services are an excellent option for the rapid transmission of documents, samples and all types of small, urgent shipment. In addition to offering speed, this new type of operator will look after the shipment from door to door.

The prices charged by the express operators are almost always more expensive than traditional groupage services operated by freight forwarders, but the express tariffs are easier to understand. Companies which send larger consignments (over 500 kilos) through the express operators must be prepared to pay the equivalent of the price for a full load trailer. So despatching 500 kilos to Paris might cost the exporter as much as if he had booked a full trailer, capable of carrying 24,000 kilos, from a traditional freight forwarder. The rate schedules of the express operators include all incidental charges, such as customs clearance, and are clearly set out. The professional presentation of the express companies, together with the simplified price structure and the enhanced service levels, have led to a rapid growth in demand for their services. As trading opportunities within the EC increase, this group of companies will continue to be major beneficiaries and of immense service to smaller shippers.

The traditional business of the express operator has been the 'envelope trade'. This is the urgent transmission of documents on behalf of a wide variety of customers. The growth of fax services has meant that much of this business can now be transmitted electronically. As a reaction to this development, the express operators are now ready to take heavier consignments, formerly the traditional preserve of the freight forwarder. A report published in January 1989 by the Institute of Distribution and Logistics Management forecast a rise of 40 per cent per year in express traffic between 1988 and 1992, and the express operators are in a good position to capture a substantial proportion of this growth.

Much of the traffic attracted to the express operators was previously carried by the airlines who are now themselves beginning to market competitively priced services in an effort to regain some of this business. Air freight forwarders, the traditional supporters of the scheduled airlines, are also now entering the door-to-door market as a response to the express operators. Many freight forwarders, too, have launched express services between the UK and the rest of Europe. Operationally, many forwarders are quite competent at organising the delivery of goods within 24 or 48 hours, and they make their services attractive by offering far lower rates than the express companies. The marketing razzmatazz which the express operators engender to promote their products is quite alien to the majority of freight forwarders, so the latter have a major problem in telling their potential customers about the existence of their low-cost alternatives.

The clear distinctions which used to exist between express operators, air forwarders and groupage operators are becoming blurred and the market will doubtless become more competitive.

Ro-Ro ferries

Ro-Ro ferries have transformed the transport links between the UK and the rest of Europe. Before the existence of the ferry, goods were taken to the docks and loaded aboard conventional vessels which sailed across the Channel and North Sea to the Continent. Here goods were discharged and then redelivered to the consignees by road or rail.

The principle of the Ro-Ro ferry is summed up by the term 'Ro-Ro' which means 'roll-on, roll-off'. The trailer drives on to the ferry and drives off again just like motorists who travel to the Continent on holiday. The goods remain loaded on the trailer throughout the sea crossing. All trailers travel to and from the UK on Ro-Ro ferries, and the main port is Dover which handles over 1000 trailers a day to and from the Continent.

There are now dozens of Ro-Ro services (Appendix 1) between the UK, the Continent and Scandinavia. The main ports are on the east and south coasts of England. Apart from Dover, other major Ro-Ro ports include Felixstowe, Hull, Poole and Plymouth in England; Calais, Dunkirk, Ostend and Zeebrugge on the Continent.

Normally, the choice of route will be left to the trailer operator or freight forwarder, and the decision will be taken in the light of operational requirements, the price of the ferry crossing and other factors. The variety of routes means that freight forwarders have a wide choice of options. New services start up and others close down at regular intervals and the forwarders have to keep up to date with developments.

The biggest threat facing the Ro-Ro shipping lines is the Channel Tunnel which will, for the first time, provide an alternative method of crossing the Channel (see Chapter 13).

Accompanied or unaccompanied trailers

Trailers are shipped across the Channel or North Sea either accompanied or unaccompanied. When a trailer travels accompanied, this means that both the trailer and the tractor travel together, and the driver takes the vehicle on and off the ferry. Unaccompanied trailers travel alone which means that the driver leaves the unit on the quayside, and the shipping companies organise the loading and the unloading of the trailers. This procedure is carried out by using tug masters which are small tractors capable of pulling trailers on and off ships. When the trailer arrives on the Continent, another tractor and driver will collect it and take the unit to its destination.

In general terms, most accompanied trailers use the Channel ports where the journey is relatively short, although even on these routes there are a substantial number of unaccompanied units. Longer routes, in either time or distance, tend to be dominated by unaccompanied traffic because hauliers do not want to pay drivers for sitting on a ship or have their tractor unit immobilised for a long period.

The larger hauliers favour unaccompanied trailers over accompanied units. Operating an unaccompanied service requires a high degree of organisational skill and larger companies have invested in depot networks and opened Continental offices, so that the trucking of the trailers can be organised on both sides of the Channel. Smaller companies prefer to send their trailers driver-accompanied if only because they have no arrangements for the handling of unaccompanied units.

From the user's point of view there is no real difference between either type of trailer services operation. Some companies will insist that driver-accompanied operations are more efficient because the presence of a driver at all times ensures a minimum of delay at the ports. A driver can shout (and swear!) while an unaccompanied trailer will not complain if it is left in a corner for a few days.

However, as long as the unaccompanied operator has organised an efficient operation, there is no reason for any delay. The large hauliers, including such well-known names as Ferrymasters, MAT Transport and Norfolk Line, have well-oiled operations which handle large numbers of unaccompanied trailers every day with great efficiency. Large hauliers also provide a driver-accompanied alternative which may be appropriate for certain specific traffic flows. A further advantage of unaccompanied trailer movements is that they can take advantage of night and weekend sailings. Trailers can arrive at a port, such as Hull, in the early evening and catch one of the overnight ferries which take about 12 hours to reach the Continent. Trailers can also be sent on ferries which travel at unsocial hours through the night.

Transport by trailer

With the development of the motorway system throughout Europe, the road trailer has become the most favoured method of moving goods. The advantage of the trailer, compared with other forms of transport, is that goods can be loaded on to a unit in one place and unloaded from the same trailer at their destination. This means that handling *en route* is avoided and thus the risk of damaging goods is also reduced. In addition, virtually every factory or warehouse in Europe is situated on a road so trailers can collect and deliver goods anywhere.

No other form of transport has such versatility. To send goods by air or by rail, you must move them to the airport or railway station unless you have the good fortune to have a factory or warehouse which is rail-connected.

Types of trailer

Tilt trailer

The most popular trailer used for transport in Europe is the tilt trailer (Figure 3.1), often colloquially referred to as a 'tilt'. Its name comes from the tarpaulin cover which encloses the goods and protects them against the weather. The legal name for this vehicle is a semi-trailer. The whole tilt can roll back the length of the trailer for loading and unloading purposes. The tilt rests on a series of wooden supports which ensure that the tilt does not bow.

In addition to the tilt which unrolls, the wooden supports of the vehicle can also be removed fairly easily. This is useful when the cargo is a large indivisible piece which requires a crane to manoeuvre the goods on to the unit. It also means that, without the wooden supports, goods can be loaded through the top of the trailer.

Yet in most cases, the tilt and the wooden supports can remain fixed to the trailer, as goods can be loaded on to the trailer once the two flaps at the back of the tilt have been opened. Goods can then be loaded manually or a forklift truck can drive on to the tilt carrying a pallet. The floor of a tilt trailer is wooden but increasingly nowadays the floors are reinforced with galvanised steel.

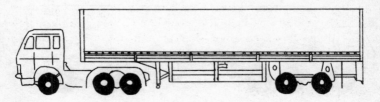

Figure 3.1 *A 12 metre tilt trailer and tractor*

Anyone who drives on motorways will see tilt trailers every day, and to the untrained eye they all look similar. In fact, as with private cars, there are many different types and models available, and hauliers choose the appropriate model to meet their requirements.

The standard length of most tilt trailers travelling in the UK is 12.2 metres. The emphasis in recent years has been on lengthening the tilt as much as possible, while still complying with the regulations. From 1 January 1990 the maximum permitted length for new semi-trailers is 13.6 metres. Trailer manufacturers are equally interested in maximising the internal height of the tilts and the newer models tend to be 2.5 metres high. The weight limits have not changed, so the new longer trailers, which will gradually make their appearance on UK roads during the next few years, are intended to take additional lighter-weight goods.

The internal dimensions of tilts are about 12.2 metres long by 2.4 metres wide and 2.5 metres high. With the introduction of the longer tilts from January 1990, the internal length of new trailers will be 13.3 metres. If the precise measurements are a critical factor, the only option is to ask the nominated haulier for a precise specification of their trailers.

Box trailers
A variation of the tilt trailer is the box trailer (Figure 3.2), also known as a box van. The carrying unit is a box with solid sides and doors. Box trailers are used to transport fragile consignments such as data processing, electrical or electronic equipment. Because all sides of the unit are solid, the goods are well protected and may require less packing as a result. A box trailer can only be loaded through the back doors. As the sides of some units are made of a solid material, the carrying capacity of box trailers is often less than for tilts. This is not normally a problem as the type of goods suitable for box trailers is usually relatively light.

Flat trailers
A flat trailer (Figure 3.3), often referred to as a flat bed trailer, is a standard

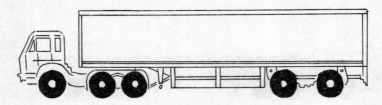

Figure 3.2 *A 12 metre box trailer and tractor*

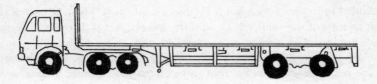

Figure 3.3 *A 12 metre flat trailer and tractor*

trailer which does not have a tilt. Goods are transported either totally unprotected or covered with a sheet which is normally filthy! The sheet provides limited protection against rain but not nearly the high level of shelter afforded by the tilt trailer. Flat trailers, known colloquially as 'flats', are used for goods which do not require any great degree of protection; for example, steel bars or ingots. Flats are also used for goods which, because of their size, cannot be loaded on to a standard tilt trailer.

Small shippers are unlikely to come across flat trailers, as they are generally used for larger consignments. Flat trailers should not be used for the transport of goods susceptible to damage through the ingress of water or moisture.

The great advantage of all these trailers is the operational flexibility which they provide for both traders and hauliers. All these types of trailer have retractable legs which can be wound down and can support the whole unit. This means that companies which require a few hours to load or discharge a trailer can request that the trailer is left at their premises. The tractor will depart, and return a few hours later, and the standing charge for the trailer will be modest. Relatively, the expensive piece of equipment is the tractor unit, and most hauliers are far more anxious to ensure that their tractors are on the move than their trailers.

Draw-bar trailer
An increasingly popular form of road vehicle within Europe is the draw-bar trailer (Figure 3.4), also known as a road train. A draw-bar unit is an

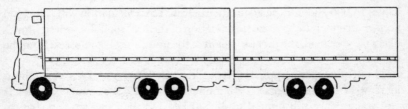

Figure 3.4 *A draw-bar trailer*

extended tilt trailer which has been divided into two. The first part of the unit consists of the rigid vehicle and the second part is a trailer. The two parts are linked by a solid coupling device.

Users of draw-bar trailers will not notice any difference in the internal structure between a draw-bar unit and a tilt trailer. The length of each part is substantially less but the overall draw-bar unit can be as long as 18 metres. Within the overall limitation, individual manufacturers choose how long each part will be for maximum operating efficiency.

The popularity of draw-bar units has increased as they are suitable for shipping large numbers of small packages and they provide operators with additional flexibility. The unit can be split in two with the back half hitched to another rigid vehicle for onward movement. Alternatively, the back part of the unit can be dropped for a few hours for goods to be loaded while the front vehicle continues and completes other jobs.

Specialised equipment
From time to time exporters or importers require specialised equipment to transport very heavy goods, very light goods or goods with out-of-gauge dimensions. Goods which are both extremely heavy and high will require a 'low loader'. This vehicle has a low platform and many wheels to make it capable of carrying heavy shipments.

Voluminous cargo, such as tissue paper or plastic items, can be put into a super cube trailer. This trailer has a low floor but the superstructure is very high. The wheels are small so only light goods can be put into the unit. The design of the trailer allows shippers to maximise the carrying capacity of the unit – invaluable if the product is both light and bulky.

Axle weights
The carrying capacity of tilt or flat trailers depends on the number of axles on each trailer. The rules vary throughout the EC, and the weight limits include an allowance for the weight of the trailer and tractor. The maximum legal weight allowed in the UK is 38 tonnes, and the combined tractor and trailer must have a total of five axles – two plus three or three plus two. The tractor and trailer together weigh about 14,000 kilos, so this leaves 24,000 kilos for the goods themselves. This calculation will change in accordance with the precise specification of the unit so, if the weight limit is likely to be critical, the precise weight of the units must be obtained from the carrier.

The 38 tonne limit applies to five-axle combinations, and the weight limit increased from 32.5 tonnes to 38 tonnes on 1 May 1983. Four-axle trailers and tractors are still limited to 32,520 kilos, so their carrying capacity is limited to between 18,000 and 20,000 kilos. Since the legislative changes, most new trailers have three axles, so are capable of carrying 38,000 kilos – older trailers are likely to be of the two-axle type. Draw-bar trailers, although longer than any other vehicle, are limited to 32,500 kilos, and this removes some of the advantages which might be gained from their additional length.

Other countries of the EC generally have higher weight limits than the UK, and the other member states have standardised on 40,000 kilos. This is a politically controversial issue; many British people do not like the prospect of even heavier vehicles on the roads. On the other hand, the more cargo that can be carried, the lower the number of lorries – another factor to be considered.

The UK has successfully obtained a postponement on any changes to its current weight limits which will last until 1999. Ostensibly, this extension has been granted to allow sufficient time for the UK government to organise the strengthening of road bridges. It is possible that the proposed changes will be introduced before 1999 – in any case most of the newer vehicles are already plated for 40 tonne operations.

Full load traffic

When goods have to be sent to another part of Europe by road trailer, the shipment can be classified in one of three ways – as a full load, a part load or a groupage shipment. A full load is when the goods occupy the whole of the trailer meaning that the vehicle runs from consignor to consignee entirely on your behalf.

A full load shipment cannot be delineated in terms of weight or volume except to state that the trailer space or capacity is occupied by the one consignment. If the goods are heavy, the cargo is likely to weigh between 16,000 and 24,000 kilos whereas light goods, such as plastic goods, fill the capacity of the trailer even if the weight of the cargo is negligible.

Part load traffic

When a substantial proportion of the trailer is taken up by one shipment, the consignment is usually referred to as a part load. A haulier will combine between two and five part loads together, although there is no firm rule about this. The traffic is all destined for a similar area and, in most cases, a part load shipment weighs anything from 3000 to 15,000 kilos or occupies a similar capacity of the trailer in volume terms. Hauliers advertise their part load services, and shippers with regular part load business are keenly sought after by the transport industry.

Groupage traffic

Smaller shipments are normally referred to as groupage cargo. Groupage has traditionally been the preserve of the freight forwarder, although in recent years hauliers and courier companies have begun to offer similar services. Groupage operators consolidate shipments from several customers, and load them all on to trailers which run to major commercial centres overseas. Here the vehicles are unloaded and each consignment is treated separately again; final delivery is often made by a local haulier.

There are hundreds, if not thousands, of groupage services operating in both directions between the UK and other parts of Europe. Typically, to a country like France, there are groupage services operating to the major centres – Lille in the north, Paris, Lyons in the Rhône-Alpes region, Marseilles in the south and Bordeaux in the west. Other centres are also served by companies which have managed to build up a good base traffic to a specific destination, but most groupage services link major commercial centres. In the UK the major groupage centres are London, Birmingham, Bradford/Leeds, Manchester and Glasgow. Services also depart from other towns where forwarders promote themselves on the basis that freight can be handled much more quickly in smaller centres.

For small businesses, groupage services are likely to be more important than either full or part loads. The companies which offer groupage services need to invest in a depot network, delivery vehicles and competent receiving and despatching agents abroad. The alternative, which is widely practised, is to sub-contract the complete operation, but this option still requires a strict control of depots and hauliers as well as long-term contractual arrangements with companies supplying these services. The forwarders provide a door-to-door service, so they need to have the capability of arranging the collection and delivery of small consignments in any part of the country.

There is no typical groupage shipment but the term covers anything over about 10 kilos in weight up to about 5000 kilos. Freight forwarders who are reputable and competent groupage operators normally offer several departures each week to major destinations and, in some cases, services run every day. There might be only one departure per week to less popular destinations. These freight forwarders run their groupage services to a timetable, so a trailer to Paris might leave on a Monday, Wednesday and Friday, a trailer to Lille on a Tuesday and Friday and a trailer to Lyons on a Friday only. This allows exporters and importers to plan their despatches and so avoid their goods standing in a depot unnecessarily.

As a rule of thumb, most groupage services tend to depart at the end of a week, as this is when exporters have finished producing the goods. Trailers then travel over a weekend and can be in most other parts of Europe on the Monday or at the latest on Tuesday morning. The advantage of a weekend transit is that the shipper is making use of what is normally 'dead time' rather than having the goods move during the working week when they could be used for production or sale.

There are several regular publications which provide up-to-date information about groupage services (Appendix 2); these should be consulted before contacting the freight forwarders directly.

Pricing of trailer services

The smaller the consignment, the higher the freight charge, relatively speaking. If a trailer from London to Paris costs £600, the full load customer can expect to pay about £700 for 20 tonnes or £35 per 1000 kilos. The part load shipper with 10 tonnes will not pay half, but perhaps two-thirds of the selling price – about £470, or £47 per 1000 kilos. The groupage shipper who comes along with 1000 kilos can expect to pay around £130 which represents 18.5 per cent of the cost for perhaps 6 per cent of the capacity of the trailer.

This explains why freight forwarders are enthusiastic promoters of groupage services as opportunities exist for making substantial profits. Many exporters and importers are, however, embarrassed about approaching a freight forwarder with a small shipment of, say, 20 kilos. This is quite an unnecessary attitude as freight forwarders are extremely interested in attracting as many small shipments as possible as their profitability climbs steeply once they have reached the break-even weight.

Yet before condemning freight forwarders for profiteering from groupage services, it must be remembered that the overheads and financial risks of running a groupage service are considerable. The forwarder has to invest in the infrastructure, promote the service and, above all, maintain the schedule. The reliable forwarder, if advertising a three times per week service, will leave three times each week even if there is insufficient cargo. To run an economical groupage service, a minimum of about 8000 to 9000 kilos is required to ensure a profit, and groupage operators will think nothing of departing with less than 1000 kilos so that the service is maintained and customer confidence retained.

Container services

Before the era of the road trailer, containers (see Chapter 5) were widely used to transport goods between the UK and the rest of Europe. Then the trailer became dominant and use of the container declined. In recent years, however, the container operators have made a spirited, successful effort to regain their market share. With the opening of the Channel Tunnel, planned for June 1993, container traffic will receive another boost.

The well-known container operators within Europe include Bell Line, Geest North Sea Line, IFF and Seawheel. These companies provide an integrated door-to-door service which includes collection and delivery as well as shipment across the North Sea. The container operators tend to use the east coast ports, principally Felixstowe and Ipswich. Containers are almost always shipped unaccompanied which means that the actual containers are lifted off their chassis at the port of departure and then put back on another chassis at the port of arrival.

The transit time for containers used to compare unfavourably with that for trailers. The differential has narrowed, and in many cases disappeared completely, as the container companies now also ensure daily sailings across the North Sea so that they can compete with their rivals in road haulage. The container companies also favour the use of rail, both in the UK and on the Continent, for longer journeys. Some of the companies are large users of the barge services which ply down the River Rhine and link Rotterdam with the industrial heartland of Germany.

Types of container

The types of container used for intra-European transport are the same as those used for deep-sea traffic (Chapter 5). The commonest types are 20 and 40 feet, and this refers to the length of the container.

The majority of containers open at the rear, so loading and unloading can become time-consuming. On the other hand, containers have solid sides so they offer better protection than trailers, especially against rain. There are various specialised types of container (see Chapter 5) which have been designed to cater for specific requirements.

One of the reasons why containers have increased in popularity is that the container companies have managed to increase the internal width and height of containers. Previously, the internal size of a container was smaller than that of a trailer but this is no longer the case. Individual container sizes vary from one manufacturer to another, so when a precise specification is required, the safest course of action is to contact the container operator and obtain the dimensions.

Rail freight

Rail freight within Europe should only be used in special circumstances and, for most types of cargo, rail freight is an inappropriate method of transport. British Rail will naturally demur at this conclusion, but rail freight is only suitable for large quantities of heavy or bulky goods.

Commodities which move by rail include coal, steel, bulk chemicals and other heavy items. The advantage of rail freight is that the weight restrictions imposed on road vehicles do not exist, and there are specialised goods wagons now available which can carry up to 63 tonnes of freight.

Small shippers, however, are unlikely to have such vast quantities of goods to move at the same time. For small individual packages, British Rail does offer an international service, but in terms of transit time it cannot compete with the road groupage operators.

The other requirement for freight is the existence of a private siding, preferably at both ends of the journey. In the UK private sidings are not very common, except with large regular shippers, although on the Continent, particularly in Germany and Switzerland, private sidings are more widespread. The existence of a private siding allows the wagon to go from door to door, avoiding delays and expensive handling charges at goods depots.

Companies which are likely to be moving large quantities of goods can obtain a grant towards the building of a private siding. The grant comes from the Department of Transport under Section 8 of the Transport Act 1968.

The role of rail will also change considerably on completion of the Channel Tunnel. In theory, British Rail, together with its European counterparts French Railways (SNCF) and Belgian Railways (SNCB), will be able to provide an express service for small packages using the Tunnel. The problem facing British Rail will be to overcome years of mistrust about its standard of service and convince shippers that goods will arrive on time and undamaged. The legacy of poor publicity will not be easily surmounted.

Own account operations

In contrast to the domestic market, own account operations are quite rare in international transport. Some companies do send their own vehicles abroad but few small firms are advised to follow this course of action. In almost every case, sending one's own vehicle will be a great deal more expensive than entrusting the consignment to a freight forwarder. It is rare for an own account operator to have a back load and, as they are forbidden to canvass for commercial work overseas, the own account operator is inevitably faced with travelling empty for one leg of the journey. In addition, an occasional shipper will have to pay a much higher sea freight rate for the ferry than an established haulier, although a small discount will be available if the sea freight is booked through a regular user of the ferry services.

41

Great care must be taken with documentation. Any mistake in the documents will result in the vehicle being immobilised for hours or even days, and an inexperienced driver will not know where to turn for assistance. Even if a company decides to send their own vehicles abroad, they are strongly advised to entrust all the documentation to an established freight forwarder who can also provide the addresses of other reputable forwarders in all the countries on the route.

In certain circumstances, sending one's own vehicle is the only option, and this is when careful preparation is required. For an exhibition or an emergency shipment, the only alternative may be to hire a vehicle from one of the rental companies and drive over to the Continent. The recommendation is to try to avoid this eventuality but, if it does arise, do seek professional help from a forwarder whose small fee will save a great deal of trouble at a later stage.

Chapter 4

Overseas Transport by Air

The main trading partners of the UK

USA
Trading links with the USA have been traditionally strong and while American multinationals used to establish factories and distribution companies in the UK, it is now British companies which establish American subsidiaries. Transport links with the USA are excellent and goods can be sent easily by sea or by air. The main trap for the unwary is to underestimate the distances within the USA. For example, goods destined for California should not be sent via New York, as New York is only half-way there. Transport between the east and west coasts of the USA is simple to organise, but the cost of the internal movement can easily be greater than the cost of sending the shipment across the Atlantic. Mastery of the American market depends on looking at a map before organising the transport.

Far East
The Far Eastern countries are important trading partners, and the links between the UK and what are now referred to as the Pacific Rim countries will expand in the future. The economic giant of the area is Japan whose electronic gadgets, photographic goods and motor cars are seen in every high street in the UK. Yet Japan is now buying an increasing quantity of goods from the UK as its consumers acquire a taste for Western products.

Behind Japan stand the newly industrialised countries which include Taiwan and South Korea, as well as the great trading centres of Hong Kong and Singapore. All these countries are enormous importers and exporters whose economic power grows every year.

Middle East
Following the oil crisis of 1973–74, the economic importance of the oil states of the Middle East increased, and many countries in the region bought large quantities of goods from the UK. The fall in the price of oil, combined with the effects of the prolonged Iran/Iraq war, curtailed growth opportunities. Some countries, such as Kuwait or Saudi Arabia, import considerable

43

volumes of cargo from the UK, but their buying habits are vulnerable to fluctuations in the price of oil and changes in the exchange rate.

Rest of the world
The once traditional trading partners of Australia, New Zealand, India and South Africa are important, particularly for certain commodities. But their relative importance for UK trade has declined, and this makes the options for transport more limited. Arranging transport to some of the smaller trading partners in Africa or Asia can sometimes be difficult as choice is limited.

Air freight

The quickest method of sending goods to another continent is by air, and it is also the mode of transport which is expanding at the fastest rate. Apart from limitations on the size of individual consignments and on the carriage of hazardous goods and explosives (see Chapter 8), there are no goods which cannot be carried by air. There are, however, certain types of cargo which are particularly well suited to air freight. These include fresh fruit and flowers, livestock, perishable goods, fashion goods and newspapers, as well as small high-value items such as diamonds, jewellery and electronic components. Emergency medical supplies or spare parts for a machine breakdown are also ideal for air freight as time is the prime consideration.

Air freight compared with sea freight
The advantage of despatching goods by air is speed. However, speed comes at a price and air freight is generally much more expensive than sea freight. This is particularly the case for larger shipments; many aircraft only have a capacity for 15 to 20 tonnes, so a consignment of such a weight involves the shipper in paying high freight charges. In comparison, a similar shipment by sea represents one container out of the hundreds or even thousands loaded on to a vessel.

The value of the consignment is a vital consideration; high-value products can absorb the higher costs of air freight much more easily than low-value commodities. The price differential between sea and air transport narrows for smaller consignments, and when the consignment weighs less than about 50 kilos there is probably not a great deal to choose in terms of price, so shippers might as well obtain the speed of air freight.

Comparison in terms of price alone is, however, not the intelligent way to choose between the methods. The main growth in air freight has arisen from the realisation that greater speed means that payment can be demanded earlier. In addition, stock levels can be much lower as the replacement of goods takes only a few days. Insurance for goods in transit is also cheaper when journey times are reduced. A shipper who sends goods to Australia will have to allow for a door-to-door transit time of six to eight weeks by sea; by air, this is reduced to about a week, so the customer receives the consignment six weeks earlier. This allows the exporter to demand and expect payment for the goods much earlier. Depending on the financial position of the company, the exporter might use bank overdraft facilities to finance overseas sales, and quicker transport which leads to quicker payment will then reduce the interest payments. The buyer also benefits as the goods can be marketed earlier. These costs can be set against the higher cost of air freight, and in many cases the higher transport charges can be justified in terms of better cash flow.

Packing requirements for air cargo are also generally less onerous than for sea freight. The reason for this is that air freight is far quicker and handling techniques gentler. Air freight traffic may be moved on a forklift truck but the use of a crane is far less likely. Sea freight cargo will almost certainly stand on a quay, exposed to the weather, for a few days, and the changes in climate are also more dramatic. Generally, packing for air transport can be lighter and any savings in packing costs can be used to pay the almost inevitably higher freight charges.

Transit time

One of the myths of air freight is that shipments are moved immediately and delays do not occur. Unless some special arrangements have been made, which might include despatch by a dedicated courier, most air freight will remain at an airport before despatch for at least a few hours. Often the delay can be due to scheduling as not every destination is served every day, and remoter places may only be linked by one or two flights each week, even from a major airport like Heathrow.

Time will also be lost if the cargo is being transhipped, so goods being flown or trucked down from Glasgow to Heathrow to a connecting flight will be delayed for some hours if only to await the departing aircraft. Shippers also need to allow time for the freight forwarder to complete customs formalities (see Chapter 6), book the freight with the airline and deliver the goods to the warehouse.

The problems of delay are even more important for import traffic, particularly when the goods transit through Gatwick or Heathrow airports. The growth in freight has outpaced the cargo-handling facilities and the cargo-handling system is frequently overloaded. The result is that importers must allow at least one day for customs clearance of non-perishable goods, and often customs formalities will take two or three days to complete. A further day is then required to organise and effect delivery, so that importers may wait for up to five days for goods to be delivered once they have arrived in the UK. Add to that the time the consignment takes to travel and shipments from the USA or Far East can easily take five to eight days from door to door. This is still much faster than sea freight but not quite as rapid as one might expect.

The choice between air and sea freight is not simple. Apart from assessing the transit time, schedules and the convenience of each method of transport, it is important to consider cash flow and other implications. All these elements come together in a theory which is called Transport Distribution Analysis (see Chapter 12).

Carriage of freight

Freight is normally loaded into the hold of an aircraft which is beneath the passenger floor. This is known as the 'belly', and is a cavernous area much smaller than the passenger deck. The internal dimensions vary from one aircraft to another, but for long distance freight traffic the Boeing 747 is the most popular aircraft. The belly of the 747 can carry motor vehicles but the internal height is only just over 1.5 metres.

Most air freight shipments, however, tend to be smaller, and they are loaded on to Unit Load Devices (ULDs) which are special air freight containers or pallets. The containers are made of aluminium and are designed to fit snugly into the cargo hold of an airline. The containers vary in size, depending on the aircraft for which they have been designed. These containers are often on roller floors. Their advantage is that they offer a high degree of protection to goods. Loading and unloading these containers is quick and, as all airlines are anxious to minimise the turn-round time of their aircraft, the containers can be loaded before the aircraft arrives and then simply pushed on board. Individual consignments are either packed or loaded into one container by the airline. Some goods will not fit into these containers, so they may be strapped on to a pallet which is secured by pulling a net tightly over the goods. Both pallets and containers come in different sizes depending on the aircraft in use. Some cargo can be loaded loose into the freight compartment, although this is now becoming much rarer. Airlines are anxious to maximise their freight revenue and they seek the best combination of cargo for every flight.

Scheduled airlines

Air freight is carried by scheduled airlines on passenger flights but the larger airlines also operate a proportion of their fleet as freight-only aircraft. The operating environment for air freight is changing almost continuously, and one effect is that new schedules and services are introduced every week.

A few years ago many airlines operated a large number of freight aircraft, known colloquially as 'freighters', but they were subsequently perceived as uneconomic compared with passenger aircraft. This applied, in particular, to the Boeing 747 ('Jumbo') which has a capacity of between 15 and 20 tonnes of cargo. The exact capacity available depends on the number of passengers carried on the same flight. The increase in cargo capacity resulted in the sale of many of the freighters and the pattern reverted to dependence on passenger aircraft.

The trend now is to return to using freighters, because the demand for non-stop flights restricts the amount of freight which can be carried. Thus, popular routes, such as between London and Hong Kong or Singapore, are now flown non-stop, but the freight capacity of the aircraft has been reduced to allow for more fuel. As the volume of air freight traffic has increased, airlines are reintroducing freighters for long-haul traffic. In addition, more and more attention now has to be paid to aviation security, and one method of simplifying the problem is to segregate freight and passengers on separate flights. This is not an economic solution but it removes from the airlines one source of potential terrorism.

The third type of aircraft used for air freight is the 'combi' which combines both freight and passengers. The difference between a combi and the ordinary passenger flight, which also accepts freight, is that on a combi flight some seats are removed from the passenger cabin, and the space is taken up by as much as 40 tonnes of freight. The airline can retain operational flexibility as to the exact split between passengers and freight which can vary from flight to flight.

Most scheduled airlines will undertake to carry air freight throughout the world. Even though the destination in question may not be served by the airline, it may complete the first stage of the journey before handing the shipment on to a regional carrier. This is particularly the case with the USA where the major carriers tend to serve gateways which include New York, Boston, Chicago, Dallas–Fort Worth, Detroit, Atlanta, Miami, San Francisco and Los Angeles. As the USA has thousands of smaller airports, the airline which has taken the goods across the Atlantic will then hand the shipment to another carrier who might hand it on again for the last part of the journey. Although competition among airlines for freight is intense, there is a high degree of practical co-operation which is essential if the system is to work.

The USA is such a well-served market that the options facing a shipper are bewildering. From the UK there are services operated by British airlines and American airlines. A further option is to send goods through a

Continental airline, all of which have their own networks of services. All the Continental airlines want to attract freight to and from the UK market and have arrangements to take goods by intra-European flights or by truck to their main cargo terminal. This is where a reputable air freight forwarder can help with in-depth knowledge of all the options to ensure the most efficient and cost-effective solution.

An increasing trend within the industry is for airlines to share the financial risks of launching a new service. For instance, Singapore Airlines introduced a cargo aircraft on the London/Singapore route, but half the freight capacity of the aircraft has been bought by British Airways which takes on the responsibility of filling up its half of the aircraft. This kind of arrangement is increasingly popular.

IATA airlines

Many scheduled airlines belong to the International Air Transport Association (IATA). IATA is involved with both passengers and freight and agrees on uniform standards in such areas as packaging, safety and freight rates. Almost all European and American airlines belong to IATA, but a few Far Eastern airlines, including Cathay Pacific and Singapore Airlines, do not belong. Sending freight with non-IATA airlines does not pose any problem, and the decision of some airlines to exclude themselves from IATA is not a drawback to using their services.

All-cargo airlines

Another group of airlines dedicate themselves solely to the carriage of cargo. The biggest cargo airline in the world is now Federal Express which acquired Flying Tigers in 1989. Other well-known cargo airlines include Cargolux, based in Luxembourg, Martinair, a Dutch company, and Anglo Airlines which is a British company.

The freight airlines operate scheduled and charter services. The scheduled timetable operates the same way as a passenger service, so that the airline may fly from London to New York three times a week at a specific time on specific days. The cargo airlines tend to concentrate on long-haul routes, relying on other airlines or road transport to connect with the less important destinations. Some cargo airlines belong to IATA while others choose not to.

Freight forwarders often use cargo airlines, and many companies see a great advantage in routeing cargo through a dedicated cargo carrier. For these airlines cargo is the absolute priority, whereas for the scheduled airlines a sudden rush of late passenger bookings may lead to some freight being left behind. In addition, cargo airlines can accept hazardous and dangerous shipments more easily as passengers are not being carried on the same aircraft.

Cargo airlines also specialise in charter flights which involve a company chartering an aircraft for one journey. Air charter is required when a destination is remote and there are no regular services. Air charter is also used for emergency and disaster relief. Air freight forwarders tend to charter complete aircraft more readily than direct traders, as the forwarders will group together the requirements of a number of their customers who, for example, may all be exhibitors at the same trade show overseas.

Freight rates for air freight

Freight rates are normally expressed on a per kilo basis, and for overseas destinations the rates are expressed in the currency of the exporting country. So UK exporters will normally receive quotes in sterling whereas importers will receive quotes in the currency of their suppliers. When a country's currency is not convertible, the US dollar is used. A rate might, therefore, be US$3 per kilo, so 100 kilos will cost US$300.

For airlines weight is the most important consideration. The weight/volume ratio is 6000 cubic centimetres to one kilogram for UK exports. For traffic from the USA to the UK, the weight/volume ratio is 7000 cubic centimetres to one kilogram. This weight/volume ratio can make the carriage of light, bulky cargo by air especially attractive.

The factors determining air freight rates are the type of commodity, the distance, and the normal factors of supply and demand. Commodity rates are not so popular as they were a few years ago, and Freight All Kind (FAK) rates are now widely available. An FAK rate will apply to all types of non-hazardous cargo moving between two places. Thus, freight rates from the Far East to the UK tend to be higher than for traffic moving in the other direction, as more goods are imported from that region and aircraft capacity is at a premium. Similarly, prices to remoter areas, such as West Africa or the Pacific Islands, will be higher because the choice of service is limited.

The freight rates are recommended by IATA, and they are, in theory, binding on all IATA member airlines. Non-IATA airlines can set their own pricing policies quite independently, but in reality will align their rates with their IATA competitors. Competition for air freight is, therefore, meant to be limited to questions of service rather than price, and the type of cartel which exists to govern passenger fares has been extended to include freight. In reality, there is price competition between airlines, and much of this has been stimulated by the 'open skies' policy adopted by the USA.

Governments also have a role to play as all IATA rates have to be ratified by each government.

Yet just as passengers seek out 'bucket shops' in order to buy cheaper tickets which the airlines slip to their chosen outlets, there are ways of skirting around the IATA cartel. This is where the skill and expertise of an air freight forwarder are essential. Without the support of the freight forwarders, the airlines would not have any traffic; the forwarders receive recognition for their crucial support through discounts on the published tariffs. The size of these discounts depends on the volume of cargo the freight forwarder directs at each airline, so the discounts obtained vary widely. Many airlines and forwarders will deny the existence of these discounts and negotiations are usually held in the strictest confidence between the parties concerned. Some of the discount is passed on to the customer but it also represents the freight forwarder's operating margin. The official margin for freight forwarders' commission has been set at 5 per cent.

There is also a small group of air freight wholesalers. These companies are the freight forwarders' forwarders in that they group traffic from several forwarders and then hand it over to an airline. Their bulk purchasing allows them to quote the freight forwarders very attractive rates. The wholesalers do not accept goods directly from exporters or importers.

Air freight consolidation

Freight forwarders will also organise consolidation services to certain destinations. The principle behind these consolidation services is exactly the same as for trailer groupage. The air freight forwarder will bring together goods from several different companies, load them on to one pallet or into a container, and deliver the unit to the airline. The airline will normally charge for the complete unit, whereas the forwarder will invoice each shipper for a proportion of the total cost plus a margin.

Consolidation rates, shortened frequently to consol rates, are cheaper than when goods are consigned via a forwarder directly to an airline. There are daily consolidations to nearly all the major trading centres around the world. Some forwarders offer consolidation services which use other European airlines, so goods are first taken to the Continent before on-forwarding overseas.

Finding a consolidation service to the required destination is not difficult. The large freight forwarders, with offices around the country, operate a comprehensive range of services for export and import traffic about which they will be pleased to give information. There are also specialised freight forwarders who may deal specifically in more remote or complicated markets, such as South America. This information can often be obtained by word of mouth recommendation or through the various publications (see Appendix 2). Such is the speed and pace of change within the air freight industry that it is advisable to let a dedicated freight forwarder handle traffic on your behalf. Around every airport, there are established freight forwarders who can assist with all aspects of the shipment – booking space, customs formalities, documentation and insurance as well as collection and delivery of the goods. The speed of growth of the market probably means that more and more companies will consign their goods to the air in the years ahead, so it is a method of transport which is well worth investigating.

Sea/air transport

One of the fastest growing methods of transport is sea/air and the phrase sea/air is an accurate description of it. Sea/air combines sea and air transport, normally but not necessarily in that order.

At the moment, sea/air is used primarily for traffic between the Far East and the UK, and applied to import rather than export traffic. Goods principally from Hong Kong, Japan, South Korea and Taiwan are sent by ship to another port which also has a large air freight handling capacity, and from there the cargo comes to the UK by air. Alternatively, it lands at another European airport and from there comes across to the UK by road.

The main transhipment ports used for sea/air traffic are Singapore, Vancouver, Los Angeles and Seattle on the west coast of Canada and the USA, and Dubai in the Gulf. The transit time for sea/air shipments is faster than pure sea freight and slower than air freight. Traffic from the Far East will take approximately 10 to 16 days to arrive in the UK; air freight may take two to three days, and sea freight will take about a month. In terms of price, sea/air is more expensive than sea freight, but not as expensive as air freight.

There has been an extremely rapid growth in sea/air business in recent years. The shipments tend to be larger than those sent by air freight. As there is a handling process in the middle of the journey, it is not recommended for small, delicate shipments of less than about 100 kilos in weight. The advantages for importers by sea/air are the greater speed, with the positive effect this can have on cash flow, and the price which is pitched midway between the two dominant forms of transport.

The other factor which has fuelled the growth of this method of transport is the lack of air freight capacity available from the Far East to Europe. Too many goods are fighting to be loaded on to aircraft whose capacity for freight has, in many cases, declined with the growth of non-stop services. Air carriers, particularly in the Middle East, rarely have return freight to carry to Europe, so are delighted to facilitate the passage of sea/air cargo which brings valuable additional revenue for the airlines, ports and shipping lines of the region. Both passenger and cargo airlines have become interested in this new market, and it is a form of transport which will expand considerably in the future. Almost inevitably, the same combination of sea/air will also be initiated for other trade flows when the correct set of circumstances comes together.

Chapter 5
Sea Transport – Overseas

Introduction

Goods have been traded by sea for centuries. Technology changed the methods of carriage and the engine replaced sail, but the method of carrying cargo scarcely changed until the dawn of the container revolution which began around 1960.

For Britain, as an island nation, the sea has always been important; until the arrival of air freight, every shipment had to travel across the sea at some stage, if only the Channel. Sea transport is still important, and the majority, in volume terms, of trade with Africa, North America, Asia and Australasia, is handled by ships. Either conventional, container or Ro-Ro vessels are used.

The great advantage of sea transport is that virtually any type of cargo can be sent by sea. Regulations exist to control the movement of dangerous and hazardous substances, but these products can be shipped as long as the regulations are observed. Similarly, out-of-gauge pieces or indivisible loads can be moved by sea, as there are vessels which can carry almost anything.

The adaptability of sea transport means that it is used more widely than any other method of transport. For special types of goods, particular ships are designed to ensure that the cargo is carried safely. Oil is carried in oil tankers and, apart from a pipeline, no other form of transport is appropriate – it is certainly uneconomical and impractical to carry oil in vast quantities by air.

Transit time

Shipment by sea is slow, even though in recent years the speed of ships has increased considerably. Shipping links with major markets, such as the USA, the Middle East and the Far East, are excellent, but a vessel still takes between seven and nine days to cross the Atlantic to the east coast of the USA. The transit time to the Middle East is about two to three weeks, and to the Far East between three and five weeks.

These port-to-port transit times may appear long, but every ship adheres to a timetable and calls at several ports on each trip. Thus, vessels which call in the UK will also call at Continental ports to discharge and collect cargo. The most important UK port for deep-sea traffic is Felixstowe, although other ports, including Tilbury, Liverpool and Southampton, also play an important part in overseas trade. Ships calling in the UK often call at Antwerp, Hamburg, Rotterdam or Le Havre, and every stop takes up a full day. The same procedure occurs overseas, so that vessels going to the Far East will call at Singapore, and then proceed north to Hong Kong, Taiwan, Korea and Japan.

Most shipping lines request that cargo is delivered to the quayside two or three days before departure. This allowance must be added to the transit time as must any waiting time for the vessel. The door-to-door transit time is considerably longer than the port-to-port times advertised and, if time is critical, it is important to calculate the period required realistically.

Containers

Most ships are container vessels, and the arrival of the container has transformed the deep-sea shipping market over the last 20 years. Containers of different sizes are loaded on to a vessel and unloaded at the port of destination. The container allows the exporter and importer to benefit from a door-to-door service. The container is normally placed at the exporter's factory for loading, and from there taken by road or rail to the port of embarkation. At the end of the journey, the container is delivered to the consignee for unloading.

The advantage of the container for the shipper is that the goods do not have to be handled as the whole container is lifted on and off the vessel. Packing need not be quite so rigorous as for conventional shipment, and this makes the cost of transport more economical. It also puts the burden of responsibility for loading and unloading the goods on to the consignor and consignee who are more likely to handle them carefully.

Another advantage of container transport is that security is improved – the container remains sealed throughout the journey except for customs examination. In practical terms, it is also far more difficult to spirit away a complete container than individual pieces of cargo.

Container ships now serve all the main markets of the world, and it is far easier to find container services to most destinations than conventional vessels. Container services, however, demand the existence of a supporting infrastructure which includes handling equipment and container-carrying lorries which are known as skeletal lorries. Containers are loaded on to skeletals at the port or at the railway yard nearest to the final destination of the goods.

Countries in Europe, North America and most parts of the Far East have

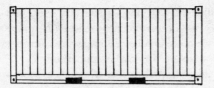

Figure 5.1 *A 20 foot container*

invested the enormous sums required in port infrastructure, but this is not the case in all other parts of the world. Certain areas of India, China and Africa do not have the technology for containerisation and this complicates the operation of container services. Absence of appropriate road equipment in some markets means that containers are unloaded or 'stripped' at the port, and the goods are put on to local lorries for final delivery. This defeats one of the great objectives of containerisation – the door-to-door movement concept. However, the precise state of the capability of different countries to handle containers is changing all the time, and the importance of the container is still increasing.

Types of container – 20 and 40 foot

In the deep-sea trades containers are often colloquially referred to as 'boxes'. The shipping lines refer to containers as either 20 footers (Figure 5.1) or 40 footers (Figure 5.2). In articles and on documentation the words are usually written as 20′ or 40′.

The 20′ and 40′ refer to the length of the container, and in most trades shippers can choose only between these two possibilities. On certain routes, 35′ containers are available, and there is the possibility that 60′ containers will be introduced in the future. For practical purposes, however, choice is limited to the 20′ and 40′ options.

Like trailers, the precise internal dimensions of containers vary depending on the manufacturer. As a general rule, the internal width of a container is 2.2 metres and the internal height 2.3 metres. Shipping lines have been

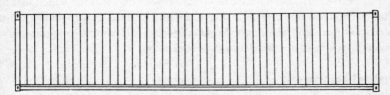

Figure 5.2 *A 40 foot container*

anxious to maximise the carrying capacity of containers, particularly the internal height, so units built recently tend to be more spacious than the older ones. When absolute precision is important, it is essential to check with the shipping line or freight forwarder concerned.

Containers are made from a variety of metals so some are heavy and some light. This is one of the factors which influences their carrying capacity. A more important factor is the weight restrictions on UK roads as most containers travel by road between the factory and the port. If the road restrictions limit the weight of the cargo which can be loaded, the solution is to send the container by rail where weight restrictions do not effectively exist. This can normally be arranged through the Freightliner service. Freightliner, which is a division of Railfreight Distribution, operates a network of container trains linking the main ports, including Southampton and Felixstowe, with the main UK industrial and commercial centres. The use of Freightliner allows shippers to load heavier cargo into the container, except that the first part of the journey between the factory and railhead may still be by road, in which case the weight restrictions, applicable to road movements, will still be valid.

The framework of a 40' container is heavier than a 20', not least because more material is used to build the container. This means that, in certain cases, 20' containers can accept a higher payload than 40' containers, but this again depends on the age and manufacture of the box. As a general rule, 20' containers can accept between 18,000 and 20,000 kilos of goods and 40' containers between 17,000 and 18,500 kilos. There are, however, plenty of exceptions to these generalisations and, if the weight limit is of critical importance, the freight forwarder or shipping line should be consulted.

A full container load, whether a 20' or a 40', is referred to as an FCL. Shipping a 40' FCL will always be more expensive than shipping a 20' FCL as it occupies more space on the vessel. In most cases, the 40' price will be double the 20' price, but on certain routes the 40' rate may be only one and a half or one and three-quarters the 20' price or in some cases more than double the 20' rate. These differences arise because every shipping line has to match its containers to demand, and in some trades demand for 20' or 40' boxes is greater in one direction than the other.

For deep-sea traffic, most of the containers are end-loading which means that the doors at one end of the box open and all cargo has to be loaded or unloaded through these doors. Forklift trucks, used widely for loading and unloading, can easily drive into the containers.

Special equipment
Shipping lines are aware of the need to have special types of container which can carry cargo unsuitable for the standard units. Almost inevitably,

shipping lines make a substantial surcharge for specialised equipment; this reflects the fact that the containers are not so readily available and special handling is required.

Flat rack containers

These containers can be used for the shipment of machinery which will not fit into a standard box. The container has a base with very short sides. The machine or piece of equipment is not given total protection from the weather, as normally some parts of the machine will protrude out of the flat rack, thus making the use of such a container essential. High pieces of equipment often require movement in a flat rack. As well as paying a surcharge for the container, shippers will be expected to pay for any additional space next to the flat rack which cannot be used in the normal way.

Open top containers

Open top containers are perfectly described by their name. The container has no top at all so its main use is for over-height pieces of equipment. Some shipping companies will drape a plastic or canvas sheet over the top of the goods, but this type of cover provides only minimum protection.

Removable roof containers

Removable roof containers must not be confused with open top containers. The roof of the box can be removed so that goods can be loaded from overhead – useful for large machines. Once loaded, the roof goes back on to the container, and the shipment is afforded a much higher degree of protection than in an open top container. Removable roof containers have lost much of their popularity in recent years, mainly because it can be awkward to secure the roof back on to the container once it is loaded. This technical drawback has never been totally overcome and has dimmed the attraction of the removable roof container.

Refrigerated containers

Refrigerated containers are used for the transport of fresh and perishable goods, mainly foodstuffs. The containers are easily recognisable from the refrigerating unit which is attached to one end of the box. This unit maintains the cargo at a constant temperature throughout the journey which may last several weeks. All the meat imported from Australia and New Zealand is shipped across in refrigerated containers.

LCL traffic

Smaller companies are more likely to have smaller quantities of goods to ship, and so they will be looking for an LCL or less than container load service. This can apply to any size of shipment from a few kilos up to 15,000 kilos. There are LCL services linking the UK with most industrial centres overseas, so sending a small package by sea should not present any real problem.

LCL services operate in the same way as trailer groupage services with other parts of Europe (see Chapter 3). Shipments are assembled in strategically located depots around the country, and then loaded into one container which is sealed and delivered to the quayside for onward movement by sea. Upon arrival the procedure is repeated; the container is unloaded on the quayside or in a central depot and the goods are then cleared through customs and delivered to the consignee.

Shipping lines are keen to encourage LCL services. Many lines operate their own LCL services, so shippers can contact the line and be advised of service details, depot location and the rates. The other method of finding a consolidation service is through a freight forwarder – freight forwarders tend to regard LCL services as very much their preserve.

The number of consolidation services offered by freight forwarders is enormous and always subject to change. To find the most appropriate consolidation service to meet your requirements, study the freight press or ask for a recommendation from other shippers. Established freight forwarders provide regular departures to many countries around the world, so finding an efficient and reliable operator should not be difficult. Where remote destinations are concerned, the choice is more limited.

The decision whether to book directly with the shipping line or through a freight forwarder is one which has to be taken at an early stage. Booking through a shipping line means that the trader has a direct link with the carrier. But freight forwarders offer more flexibility as they are not committed to one shipping line. In addition, booking through a freight forwarder should be no more expensive than booking direct. Shipping lines often charge sea freight according to the type of cargo carried, so more valuable items pay a higher sea freight. Freight forwarders will usually charge a standard rate for non-hazardous goods, and their volume of business with the shipping line can often make their rates cheaper.

Sea freight rates for LCL cargo are always expressed in terms of the weight to measurement ratio. For sea freight this ratio is 1 cubic metre (cbm) equalling 1 metric tonne. A rate might, therefore, be expressed as £100 w/m. This means that every 1000 kilos or 1 cbm will cost £100. A consignment weighing 600 kilos but with dimensions of 2.5 cbm will therefore cost £250.

In this example the currency has been given in pounds sterling. In fact, most sea freight rates are expressed in US dollars, and the dollars are converted into sterling at the rate applicable on the day of sailing. Many traders resent this practice which exposes their shipping costs to the vagaries of the sterling/dollar exchange rate. Nevertheless, the practice is of long standing and unlikely to change.

NVOCC services

In order to personalise and market their consolidation services, many freight forwarders operate Non-Vessel Owning Common Carrier services. This cumbersome title is always abbreviated to NVOCC. A freight forwarder will market a consolidation service under a particular name, and every document, bill of lading and invoice will refer to this marketing name. For example, a forwarder may decide to call his service 'XYZ' so the bill of lading will be headed as an 'XYZ bill of lading'. In fact, the shipping line XYZ does not exist, and the forwarder will be handing the cargo on to a shipping line. Yet, to protect its own position, the freight forwarder wants to control the shipment, issue its own documents and despatch consolidation boxes. This is the essence of NVOCC services which are now offered worldwide and include both full container load and less than container load services.

Like much else in shipping, the growth of NVOCC operators has not been without controversy, particularly regarding the responsibility for the cargo in case of loss or damage. Yet many large, reputable and well-established freight forwarders have been NVOCC operators for years, and using their services does not expose companies to any real risk. More care should be taken with other NVOCC operators whose financial standing may not be so secure.

Conventional cargo

Until the advent of containerisation most cargo was shipped on conventional vessels. The most widely used expression for this method of shipment is 'break bulk'. When goods are shipped conventionally or break bulk, it means that the cargo is loaded on to the ship loose. The ship will normally have several holds and the goods are stowed in these holds or on deck for the journey.

Cargo which is shipped conventionally requires far stronger packing than if the goods are containerised, particularly if the shipment is being stowed on deck exposed to the elements. Strong packing cases are essential, plus additional protection for all delicate and moving parts.

Container services are so widespread that conventional services to many parts of the world have disappeared. They still tend, however, to serve less developed countries where the ports do not have the infrastructure to handle containers. So there are conventional liner services to parts of Africa, China and Indonesia as well as remoter destinations, such as islands in the Pacific, where the volume of cargo does not justify investment in container services. Some conventional services run regularly and freight forwarders will be aware of their schedules. (They are also advertised in the trade press.) When scheduled conventional services do not run as frequently as container services, shippers may have to wait for between one and two months for a vessel. Many conventional vessels run by inducement which means that the shipping line will provide a service when sufficient cargo is available to justify a departure. Companies who use these types of service, often referred to as 'tramp' vessels, will normally be notified by the shipping company of an impending departure.

Although conventional services are increasingly rare, these types of vessel are appropriate for cargo which is unsuitable for containers. Out-of-gauge machinery, large indivisible items or long pieces of metal, such as pipes, are more suited to conventional vessels. Certain specialised types of container do exist, but conventional vessels allow the shipper to send larger quantities at one time.

Ro-Ro services

As well as the widely known Roll-on/Roll-off (Ro-Ro) services which link the UK with other parts of Europe, there are also Ro-Ro services to destinations further afield. The main purpose of Ro-Ro vessels is to bring assembled motor cars, particularly from Japan and more recently Korea, to Europe. These vessels also carry large pieces of wheeled equipment, such as bulldozers, combine harvesters and tractors. The Ro-Ro ships have spacious holds which are ideal for large items.

The main Ro-Ro services run between Europe and the Far East, as well as to the Middle East and the USA. Their priority is the transport of motor cars, so other goods are of secondary importance. This means that the best way to find space is to provide cargo for one of the return journeys for which no cars will be available.

There are Ro-Ro services which carry trailers to North Africa and the Middle East. These ships operate from ports in Southern Europe, particularly Marseilles and Genoa. The trailers take either full load or groupage traffic. As a method of transport, there are several disadvantages of using these Ro-Ro services outside Europe. The trailers have to return empty and control over the cargo can be lost once the trailer has arrived at its destination. The empty return is an unavoidable cost which the shipper has to pay, and normally conventional or containerised services will be far more economical. Nevertheless, for a valuable consignment which requires driver-accompanied delivery, Ro-Ro services are an option to consider.

Surcharges

One of the more puzzling aspects of deep-sea shipping is the existence of surcharges. On almost every service, the freight rate will be subject to at least one surcharge, often two and sometimes more. The commonest types of surcharge are referred to as CAF (currency adjustment factor) and BAF (bunker adjustment factor) surcharges.

For the shipping lines, the justification for the currency surcharge is that their revenue is expressed in US dollars, but many of their expenses are incurred in local currencies around the world. In addition, their income, although initially quoted in dollars, is then translated into local currencies for settlement by their customers. Exchange rates change all the time and the CAF takes account of these movements.

The BAF surcharge is related to the cost of bunkering or oil which is one of the most critical costs for all shipping lines. The price of oil changes frequently and the BAF surcharge follows these fluctuations.

Another surcharge, also frequently applied, is a congestion surcharge. This is intended to cover the additional costs incurred by a vessel when it is discharging at a congested port. The ship is delayed, and running costs are high even when the ship stands at anchor. Congestion surcharges will frequently apply in India as well as some parts of Africa. They are normally levied as a flat amount per container.

From time to time shipping lines introduce a war risk surcharge. This is intended to compensate the line for the higher insurance premiums which are payable when vessels are operating in a dangerous part of the world.

The arguments surrounding the CAF and BAF surcharges centre on the problems which face exporters and importers trying to calculate accurately the cost of transport. The surcharges change, often weekly, and cannot be forecast in advance. The surcharges, however, do move both up and down, and it is not uncommon for a negative CAF surcharge to apply. This means that the freight rate is reduced by the amount of the surcharge.

Understanding a surcharge

The existence of a surcharge complicates the calculation of a freight rate. Normally, a shipping line will provide the customer with a quotation as follows.

The cost of a 20′ container to XYZ is US$2000 plus BAF which is plus 5 per cent and CAF which is minus 2 per cent. There is a congestion surcharge of US$50.

To calculate the cost of the shipment, the surcharges must be included. Surcharges relate to the base rate, not the accumulated total. In the example, the calculation will be made as follows:

Base rate		US$2000
BAF surcharge +5% of US$2000	+ US$100	
CAF surcharge − 2% of US$2000	− US$ 40	
Congestion surcharge	+ US$ 50	
Subtotal		US$ 110
Total		US$2110

The price of US$2110 applies only until such time as any of the surcharges change, and this may happen the next day. At that moment the calculation has to be redone with the new figures.

This example has used easy figures but, to complicate the matter further, most shipping lines impose surcharges which run to two decimal places.

Shipping conferences

The conference system began in the nineteenth century and, despite many attempts by competitors, shippers and sometimes governments to limit their influence, shipping conferences have survived. The essence of the conference system is the co-operation of several lines to provide an integrated service on a route. The lines agree to co-operate and the agreement is enforced through a small, centralised administrative group. The shipping lines who are party to the conference hold periodic meetings at which prices, shipping schedules and slot allocations are arranged. The slot allocation arrangement determines the total number of containers which each participating line can carry, and this agreement is intended to maintain equity between the line members. The slot allocation determines the number of containers which each participating line is allowed to carry.

A further refinement of the conference system is the existence of consortia. A consortium is a group of shipping lines which work closely together. The consortium members may all operate their own ships or they may decide to pool their resources and build ships in the colours of the consortium. The consortium becomes the member of the conference, and then has an internal discussion on service levels and slot allocations. In the Europe/Far East trade, the ACE consortium groups several Far Eastern lines which provide a joint service.

When finding out the best way of shipping a consignment, importers and exporters will often be asked whether they prefer a conference or non-conference shipping line. Every line is either a conference member or decides to act as an outsider – the word frequently used to describe non-conference lines. Shippers who use a conference service will be charged the same rate whichever member line they use. This absence of price competition does not, however, prevent the line members from competing fiercely on service levels and transit times which can vary widely.

At a first glance, the conference system may seem unfair and, certainly, accusations of price fixing and unfair competition are often heard. The advantage of the system, however, is that a high level of service is maintained on every route and that the rate agreements provide price stability for shippers. In addition, the conference system also allows less popular destinations to be served, as the higher costs and inconvenience of calling at some ports are shared between a number of lines.

The other controlling factor on the conference lines is the existence of non-conference lines. Many shipping lines choose to act as outsiders or are refused entry to the shipping conference; non-conference lines are totally independent, fix their own schedules and determine their own (usually cheaper) prices. The presence of non-conference lines means that conference lines cannot become too complacent or let their prices become uncompetitive.

Non-conference lines used to have a poor reputation, and there is certainly an element of risk in using some of them. The vessels and equipment may not be as modern, and the timetable can often be inaccurate with wide deviations from the schedule. Yet many of the non-conference lines have improved their reputation and their service can compete favourably with conference operators.

There are conferences which cover services throughout the world. For example, the North Europe Atlantic Conference co-ordinates the services of several lines which sail between North Europe and the USA. Another large conference grouping is the Far East Freight Conference (FEFC) which co-ordinates activities on the important Far East/Europe trades. The FEFC members include large European-based shipping lines such as P & O, OCL and Maersk as well as newer Far Eastern shipping lines such as OOCL and Neptune Orient Line. Under the umbrella of the FEFC, these lines can co-operate on certain matters and compete in other areas. Among the powerful non-conference members who compete against the FEFC is Evergreen, a shipping line based in Taiwan and arguably now the world's largest shipping line.

The conference system has been criticised for many years, but the system does have a capacity to adapt to the changing trading environment. Because of this ability, the conferences have survived and their existence, in many practical ways, makes shipping goods overseas far easier.

Chapter 6

Export Documentation

Introduction

The acquisition of overseas customers, while in itself an achievement, is only the first step in selling goods overseas. The job is not complete until your customer has physically received the consignment and you have been paid. As much attention must be paid to the final part of the order cycle which involves completing the documentation requirements, arranging the transport and ensuring payment.

Every exporter can recall some horror story which relates to problems with documentation. Sometimes the problems are unavoidable, but in too many cases it is the exporter who has not been punctilious enough in producing the required documents.

Errors in documentation are expensive. The first consequence of a mistake is a delay to the consignment which may be held up in a warehouse under customs control in the UK or overseas. Wherever the delay, storage charges will become payable almost immediately, and these have a habit of rising disproportionately as the delay extends from days to weeks and perhaps even months.

The storage charges have to be paid in full, even if the amount seems totally unreasonable, as the warehouse operator will simply refuse to release the goods until all charges have been settled. Most customs authorities have the reserve power to seize goods which have not been cleared through customs within a certain period. These rules ensure that customs warehouses are not used for long-term storage, and in some countries these regulations are invoked when customs officers take a personal fancy to a particular shipment!

Within Europe most goods travel by trailer and are often cleared 'on wheels'. This means that the goods remain on the trailer while customs formalities are completed. If, for some reason, a trailer is held up because of a documentation error, the haulier immediately incurs additional costs. The exporter may well be charged standage for the trailer, the tractor and the driver, and this can amount to between £300 and £400 per day. The other danger of delay is the loss of confidence by the customer. In addition, any delay in delivery will immediately lead to a deferment in settlement of the invoice, so cash flow is then affected.

Although such events occur daily, there is no need for exporters to expose themselves to these additional costs. Documentation for exports is not complicated, and the number of documents which have to be prepared by the exporter himself are very few. They must, however, be completed carefully and checked before they are despatched. In many firms, the completion of forms is seen as a routine task, and the work is done by untrained, inexperienced employees who may not be aware of the potential penalties for errors.

Many of the other forms are completed by freight forwarders, hauliers, airlines, shipping lines, as well as banks and other financial intermediaries. This chapter looks at both the documents which exporters complete and those normally completed by the suppliers of transport. The financial documents, which include letters of credit and bank drafts, are well covered in another book in this series, *Export for the Small Business*, 2nd edition (Kogan Page).

Invoice

The most important form which the exporter has to prepare is the invoice and an invoice must accompany every shipment, even if the goods are being supplied free of charge. It is the basic document used in export and every other document draws on information that appears upon it.

A commercial invoice used for export does not differ greatly from one used for a domestic transaction. Certain details will always appear such as the name, address and full details of the exporter, the name and address of the consignee and a full description of the goods. Other details on the invoice will be the marks and numbers of the packages, the price and the terms of sale. An example of a commercial invoice is shown in Figure 6.1.

Frequently, exporters are asked to prepare a pro forma invoice. This document is used for quotation purposes or when payment is being made in advance, and the words 'pro forma' will appear prominently. When samples are being sent free of charge, customs authorities will require an invoice for customs purposes only. In this case the invoice is claused 'No commercial value. Value for customs purposes only.'

Normally, every invoice should contain a statement about the origin of the goods and, for trade with certain countries, it is compulsory to state the country of origin. Some customs authorities abroad also request that the contents of an invoice are expressed in the local language. The exporter will then need to ensure that the invoice is written in English as well as in the foreign language. Even when such a request is not made, exporters will gain the thanks of their customers if they supply invoices which have been prepared in two languages.

FEDERATED OFFICE SUPPLIES LTD
189 Mill Road,
RUGBY, Warwickshire OV21 1BD
Tel: (0788) 543189 Fax: (0788) 543679

North End Trading plc,
PO Box 150
Marine Parade Post Office,
9144 SINGAPORE
Republic of Singapore   5th February, 1990

QUANTITY	DESCRIPTION	AMOUNT £
1000	Ring Binders	700
1000	Lever Arch Files	750
5	Key Cabinets Series 300	550
	C.I.F. SINGAPORE	£2000

PACKED IN 50 CARTONS NOS 1 - 50   GT. WT 700 0.9 CBM.
MARKS : NORTH END TRADING SINGAPORE 1 - 50

THESE GOODS ARE OF U.K. ORIGIN.

For and on behalf of Federated Office Supplies Ltd.

Place and date of issue

RUGBY 5.2.1990

Signature

B. WORDSWORTH
(Managing Director)

Figure 6.1 *A commercial invoice*

Regulations regarding invoices vary from one country to another and they also change frequently. For up-to-date information, shippers should consult Croner's *Export Digest* which lists the documentation requirements for every country. Amendments are published monthly.

Because of UK customs regulations, it is possible to despatch goods overseas without an accompanying invoice. Frequently, exporters assemble a shipment, contact their freight forwarder and, because of an inefficient clerical system, the goods are in the despatch bay and the invoice is still in the computer system. The result is that goods are collected, sent overseas, and will almost inevitably be blocked in customs until the invoices arrive. This sequence of events happens within Europe as well as further afield and, as transit times to the Continent are so quick, it is frustrating for the consignee to have goods destined for them held at the local customs warehouse.

To avoid these problems you must ensure that no shipment ever leaves the company without an accompanying invoice. Although one copy of the invoice should normally be sufficient, freight forwarders will have to photocopy the invoice, so it is more helpful to make two or three copies available.

To a certain extent, the arrival of the fax machine should reduce customs delays. Within Europe, invoices sent by fax are generally acceptable, although the occasional awkward customs officer may object. Some customs authorities in other parts of the world will also accept a fax as a substitute for an original invoice.

Certified invoice

Many countries request that a statement about the origin of the goods is included on the invoice and that the invoice is stamped by the country's embassy in the UK. This procedure has to be followed before the goods are despatched, so time must be allowed for the invoice to be taken to the embassy.

In most cases certification will take place on the same day or within 24 hours. There is no need for the exporter to present the invoice personally; many freight forwarders offer an authorisation service for a small fee, and there are also many messenger and consular services which will undertake this job. The embassy will usually charge a fee for certifying an invoice.

Certificate of origin

The other document frequently requested is a certificate of origin (see Figure 6.2). Certificates of origin should, like certified invoices, be

CERTIFICATE OF ORIGIN

H/ 618875

1 Consignor: المرسل :

4 Consignor's ref.:

شهادة منشأ

CERTIFICATE OF ORIGIN

2 Consignee: المرسل اليه :

تشهد السلطة الموقعة بأن البضائع الوارد بيانها أدناه

The undersigned authority certifies that the goods shown below

5 originated in: منشأها :

3 Method of Transport: مرسلة بواسطة :

غرفة التجارة العربية البريطانية

ARAB-BRITISH CHAMBER OF COMMERCE

Marks and Numbers: الأرقام والعلامات	Quantity and Kind of Packages: كمية ونوع الطرود	Description of Goods: مواصفات البضاعة	6 Weight (gross & net): الوزن (الصافي والاجمالي)

غرفة التجارة العربية البريطانية

ARAB-BRITISH CHAMBER OF COMMERCE

مكان وتاريخ الاصدار

Place and Date of Issue

Issuing Authority

سلطة الاصدار

861

Arab-British Chamber of Commerce

Figure 6.2 *A certificate of origin*

completed before goods are exported. In the UK, certificates of origin are obtainable from chambers of commerce. Once completed, the certificate will also be authorised by the chamber, which will charge a fee for its intervention.

Some countries require the certificate of origin to be certified by their embassy in the UK as well as a local chamber. This means that the certificate and supporting documentation have to be taken to the embassy for authorisation. Some embassies charge a standard fee, while others base their charges on the value of the order; this can make the procedure quite expensive. There is no justification for these high charges, and they can only be seen as a form of taxation which contributes towards the high cost of maintaining an embassy in London!

Some of the Arab countries ask for a certificate of origin which has been certified by the Arab–British Chamber of Commerce. This organisation specialises in trade promotion with the Arab world.

Packing list

The packing list (see Figure 6.3) will detail the contents of a consignment. Exporters who use a computer-based system to generate invoices can produce a packing list simultaneously, and much of the information which appears on the invoice is duplicated on the packing list. The packing list contains the number and kind of packages, their contents, the net and gross weight (normally in kilograms) and the full dimensions and total size of each package. The size of a package is often referred to as its cube. All these individual items are totalled at the foot of the packing list.

PACKING LIST					
MARKS : NORTH END TRADING 1 - 50					
CARTON NUMBERS	CONTENTS	DIMENSIONS CM	TOTAL	WEIGHT KG	TOTAL
1 - 20	50 Ring Binders	450 x 100 x 150	0.34	10	200
21 - 45	40 Lever Arch Files	550 x 150 x 150	0.50	15	375
46 - 50	1 Key Cabinet	300 x 200 x 200	0.06	25	125
TOTAL 50 CARTONS			0.9 CBM		700

Figure 6.3 *A packing list*

For some shipments a packing list is stipulated as one of the conditions of fulfilling the order. When this is not the case, the decision whether to supply a packing list is left to the discretion of the exporter. As a control document, a packing list permits the goods to be checked during their journey overseas. This is particularly useful for high-value goods or goods which are attractive to pilferers; the packing list provides additional security.

Forms completed by carriers

Every mode of transport has its own separate documents as well as others which remain the same irrespective of the method of transport. For air transport, the most important document is the air waybill, referred to as the AWB. For sea transport, the most important document is the bill of lading, shortened frequently to B/L. For international road freight, the consignment note normally completed by the haulier is the CMR note (see page 73). Shippers will frequently see these documents as well as certificates of shipment.

The customs forms used for export are nearly all various parts of the SAD (*Single Administrative Document*). Yet before goods can be shipped overseas, they have to be moved from the factory to the port, depot or airport of departure, and this domestic movement is often covered by other documents.

Standard shipping note/collection note

The standard shipping note (see Figure 6.4) is used as a form of instruction and a form of receipt when goods or a container are being delivered to the quayside for shipment by sea. The standard shipping note, which is a six-part document, will be initiated by the exporter or the haulier and given to the driver when the goods are collected from the factory. The standard shipping note contains such information as a description of the goods, the destination and, most important, the name of the dock and the vessel booking reference.

Once the goods have arrived at the docks, the standard shipping note will be signed without remark unless the goods are damaged, in which case the extent of the damage will be noted. The dock handling company also uses the standard shipping note as its instructions regarding the handling of every consignment.

There is no obligation to use a standard shipping note, although its advantage is that the form is universally accepted and recognised. The alternative for hauliers and freight forwarders is to use their own collection notes which are all slightly different from one another. Collection notes are used widely for all types of cargo whatever the mode of transport or size of

© SITPRO 1987

STANDARD SHIPPING NOTE

IMPORTANT USE THE DANGEROUS GOODS NOTE IF THE GOODS ARE CLASSIFIED AS DANGEROUS ACCORDING TO APPLICABLE REGULATIONS SEE BOX 10A

Exporter	1
Customs reference/status	2
Booking number	3
Exporter's reference	4
Port charges payable by * □ exporter □ freight forwarder other (name and address)	5
Forwarder's reference	6
Freight forwarder	7
International carrier	8
For use of receiving authority only	
Other UK transport details (e.g. ICD, terminal, vehicle bkg. ref., receiving dates)	9
Vessel/flight no. and date	Port/airport of loading	10
Port/airport of discharge	Destination	11

10A The Company preparing this note declares that, to the best of their belief, the goods have been accurately described, their quantities, weights and measurements are correct and at the time of despatch they were in good order and condition, that the goods are not classified as dangerous in any UK, IMO, ADR/RID or IATA/ICAO regulation applicable to the intended modes of transport

TO THE RECEIVING AUTHORITY. Please receive for shipment the goods described below subject to your published regulations and conditions (including those as to liability)

Shipping marks	Number and kind of packages, description of goods, non-hazardous special stowage requirements	12	Receiving authority use	Gross wt (kg) of goods 13	Cube (m²) of goods 14

For use of shipping company only	Total gross weight of goods	Total cube of goods

PREFIX and container/trailer number(s) 16	Seal number(s) 16A	Container/trailer size(s) and type(s) 16B	Tare wt (kg) as marked on CSC plate 16C	Total of boxes 13 and 16C 16D

DOCK/TERMINAL RECEIPT
Received the above number of packages/containers/trailers in apparent good order and condition unless stated hereon
RECEIVING AUTHORITY REMARKS

Haulier's name

Vehicle reg. no.

DRIVER'S SIGNATURE | SIGNATURE AND DATE

Name of company preparing this note 17

Date

(indicate name and telephone number of contact)

630 *Mark X as appropriate. If box 5 is not completed the company preparing this note may be held liable for payment of port charges
Non-completion of any boxes is a subject for resolution by the contracting parties

Figure 6.4 *A standard shipping note*

TATE FREIGHT FORMS 0908 567687

LETTRE DE VOITURE INTERNATIONALE (CMR) INTERNATIONAL CONSIGNMENT NOTE

1 Sender (Name, Address, Country) Expéditeur (Nom, Addresse, Pays)	**2** Customs Reference/Status Référence/désignation pour mise en douane
	3 Senders/Agents Reference Référence de l'expéditeur/de l'agent
4 Consignee (Name, Address, Country) Destinataire (Nom, Addresse, Pays)	**5** Carrier (Name, Address, Country) Transporteur (Nom, Addresse, Pays)
6 Place & date of taking over the goods (place, country, date) Lieu et date de la prise en charge des marchandises (Lieu, pays, date)	**7** Successive Carriers Transporteurs successifs
8 Place designated for delivery of goods (place, country) Lieu prévu pour la livraison des marchandises (lieu, pays)	This carriage is subject, notwithstanding any clause to the contrary, to the Convention on the Contract for the International Carriage of Goods by Road (CMR) Ce transport est soumis nonobstant toute clause contraire à la Convention Relative au Contrat de Transport International de Marchandises par Route (CMR)

Marks & Nos. No & Kind of Packages, Description of Goods* Marques et Nos, No et nature des colis, Désignation des marchandises* **9**	Gross weight (kg) **10** Poids Brut (kg)	Volume (m³) **11** Cubage (m³)

Carriage Charges Prix de transport **12**	Senders Instructions for Customs, etc **13** Instructions de l'Expéditeur (optional)	
Reservations Réserves **14**	Documents attached Documents Annexés (optional) **15**	
	Special agreements Conventions particulières (optional) **16**	
Goods Received/Marchandises Reçues **17**	Signature of Carrier/Signature du transporteur **18**	Company completing this note Société émettrice **19**
		Place and Date; Signature Lieu et date; Signature **20**

*N8 FOR DANGEROUS GOODS INDICATE 1 CORRECT TECHNICAL NAME (PROPER SHIPPING NAME) 2 HAZARD CLASS 3 UN NUMBER 4 FLASHPOINT IF ANY) IN °C

COPY 1 SENDER COPY 2 CONSIGNEE COPY 3 CARRIER

Approved by FTA, RHA, SIT PRO UK 1981

TATE FREIGHT FORMS 0908 567687

730

Figure 6.5 *The CMR*

consignment. The collection note is an instruction to the driver to collect a certain consignment from one place and deliver it elsewhere. The information which appears on a collection note is almost standard including the relevant addresses and a description of the goods.

The CMR form

The full English translation of CMR is Convention on the Contract for the International Carriage of Goods by Road, the length of which explains why the expression is shortened to CMR! The CMR (see Figure 6.5) will be completed by the haulier and available for signature by the sender when the goods are collected. The CMR will contain all the relevant information about the load, together with details of the trailer and the carrier.

The first copy of the CMR remains with the sender, the second accompanies the goods and the third is retained by the carrier. In most cases the carrier completes the CMR note, but most of the information relates to the exporter so there is a good case to be made for the exporter filling out the CMR. The exporter is responsible for the CMR's accuracy. Upon discharge of the goods, the consignee will be asked to sign the CMR. There is room on the CMR for the exporter or importer to add any information which might assist the haulier.

Every country in Europe, including Eastern Europe, has accepted the CMR convention which regulates the responsibilities and potential liabilities of the carrier. Hauliers will frequently assure their customers that all goods are carried 'under CMR conditions', and this offers some measure of reassurance. On the other hand, CMR liability is not in any way linked with the financial standing of the company so caution is still required.

The bill of lading

One of the oldest documents used in international trade is the bill of lading. Today, the bill of lading is still an important document which is used in virtually all circumstances when goods are being shipped overseas by container or conventional vessel. The bill of lading fulfils many purposes and is also a legal document as defined in several laws starting with the Bill of Lading Act 1855 and continuing through to the Carriage of Goods by Sea Act 1971.

Bills of lading are issued by shipping lines but are now also issued by freight forwarders and by the International Federation of Freight Forwarders Association (FIATA). All bills of lading are fairly similar in appearance (see Figure 6.6) in that they are A4 size with the name of the shipping line stated prominently at the top. Details of the shipment appear in the body of the document with room for signatures at the bottom. The reverse side (see

Figure 6.6 *An ocean bill of lading*

Figure 6.7 *The reverse side of an ocean bill of lading*

Figure 6.7) is filled with line after line of conditions of carriage which become important when something goes wrong. Careful reading of the conditions would deter most people from ever handing goods over to a shipping line, so it is perhaps best to hope everything will go well and take out insurance.

The first function of the bill of lading is to act as a receipt for goods. If goods are being shipped conventionally, cargo can be checked physically as it is loaded, and the bill of lading will include full details of the number of packages and description of the goods. In the container age, the bill will simply state the container number with a declaration 'said to contain' as the shipping line will rely on the customer's information and not inspect the contents of every container.

The bill of lading is also the contract of carriage between the shipper and the shipping line. The bill will be completed only after the ship has left the port, as only then can the shipping line complete all the parts of the bill, such as the name of the vessel and the sailing date. The other reason for the reluctance of shipping lines to issue bills of lading before the vessel has sailed arises from the possibility, however remote, of the shipment not being shipped ('short shipped'). The shipping line would find itself in legal difficulties if a bill of lading had been issued and the goods were still on the quayside.

The third function of the bill of lading is as a document of title. This means that whoever holds the bill of lading can take delivery of the goods. The buyer of the goods normally presents the original bill of lading to the shipping line at the port of arrival in order to take possession of the cargo.

The procedures surrounding a bill of lading follow a similar pattern. The shipping line issues and signs the bill of lading when the vessel has sailed. Bills of lading are issued in sets, frequently two or three originals plus three copies, and the exporter can request as many originals and copies as required. The original bill is sent to the exporter and, depending on the relationship with the shipping company and the terms of sale, payment of the freight and FOB charges may be demanded before the bill is released.

Once the exporter has the bill of lading, he can send it direct to his customer overseas who will then be able to collect the goods when they arrive. Without the original bill of lading, the consignee is unable to receive the consignment.

One of the most popular ways for a foreign importer to pay for goods is by opening a letter of credit. The importer overseas instructs his bank to establish the letter of credit, which is then sent over to a UK bank. As long as the exporter meets the conditions which are set out in the letter of credit, the money will be paid.

For greater certainty of payment, importers can insist that their customers open irrevocable letters of credit whereby sanctioning any change to the terms is almost impossible. Letters of credit are a subject for study on their own, and there have been plenty of legal cases involving them.

Their role in international transport becomes important when their terms demand the presence of a certain document which must then be made available for the financial transaction to proceed. For shipments by sea, an original bill of lading is often required before the letter of credit can be presented to the bank. In these cases, the bill of lading, together with all the other documents required, is presented to the nominated bank in the UK who then processes the letter of credit. Once all the conditions of the letter of credit have been met, the consignee will receive the original bill of lading so he can take delivery of the shipment upon its arrival.

Although the procedures surrounding a bill of lading may appear complicated, once experience has been gained the system can work well. With a bill of lading, the exporter has a certain amount of security regarding the payment for goods as, without the agreement of the exporter, the consignee cannot receive them. Nevertheless, the bill of lading should not be used as a substitute for a credit control policy, as it creates problems to have a shipment stranded on a distant quayside. Even if the consignee cannot obtain the goods, the shipper eventually has to arrange for the goods to be returned home, and this involves a further freight charge as well as substantial overseas storage costs.

For the exporter, the most important point about a bill of lading is to check it for accuracy. Every detail of a bill must be correct to avoid any possible delay. If the bill of lading is being used in conjunction with a letter of credit, it is important that any particular wording requested in the letter of credit appears on the bill. In these cases it is a good idea to send a photocopy of the letter of credit to your forwarding agent, so that he can ensure full compliance with the terms of the credit.

As transit times become faster, shipping lines and exporters have to become quicker in handling bills of lading. From the UK to the east coast of the USA by sea only takes eight to ten days so, with postal delays and weekends, there is not a great deal of time for the bill of lading to travel from the shipping line to the exporter and from there over to the consignee. This problem can partly be overcome if shipping lines despatch the original bill of lading within 24 hours of the departure of the vessel. Exporters often have to use the courier companies to ensure that documents reach another continent within one or two days. At the moment, a bill of lading sent by fax is not generally acceptable by most shipping lines unless they have total confidence in the integrity of the consignor and consignee. As electronic data interchange (EDI) gathers pace (see pages 88–90), the processing of bills of lading will also speed up – information can be transmitted

77

electronically and the original bill of lading will appear on the shipper's desk.

Different types of Bill
The liner bill of lading (see Figure 6.6) is also known as the ocean bill of lading. It is issued by a shipping line after the vessel has sailed. Until the arrival of the FIATA and the freight forwarder's bill of lading, the liner bill dominated deep-sea traffic. It is still widely used and, in many parts of the world, the liner bill is perceived as having more authority than any other type. This is not necessarily the case, but the effect of this perception is for many buyers to insist on a liner bill of lading when opening a letter of credit.

Through bill of lading. It is not always possible to send goods by the same method of transport throughout their journey. For example, goods going to the USA may be unloaded in New York and then go by rail to the west coast. Alternatively, goods may be transferred from one vessel to another smaller line, and this frequently happens when the destination is more remote. Exporters do not want the complication of having to obtain two bills of lading, so shipping companies will issue the through bill of lading which covers the whole journey. The shipper only deals with the first carrier, and the exporter will be quoted a through rate. This type of bill is becoming more popular.

The FIATA combined transport bill of lading (see Figure 6.8) is a comparatively recent development, and can be seen as an effort by freight forwarders to protect their business by issuing their own bill of lading rather than passing the shipping line bill of lading on to their customers.

FIATA is an international organisation with members around the world. It will allow certain forwarders who fulfil financial and performance criteria to issue the FIATA combined transport bill of lading. One of the principal conditions for UK freight forwarders is membership of the British International Freight Association (BIFA). The advantage of the FIATA bill is that it has been accepted by the International Chamber of Commerce (ICC) which publishes the *ICC Uniform Customs and Practice for Documentary Credits*. The effect of this acceptance by the ICC is that the FIATA bill is as valid as a liner bill for all commercial transactions.

Freight forwarders will normally offer their customers a door-to-door service and the FIATA bill takes account of this type of operation, so that goods which travel by sea and rail can be accompanied by an FIATA bill throughout the journey. The freight forwarder, issuing an FIATA bill, takes full responsibility for the performance of the entire inter-modal transport as if he were the carrier. The FIATA bill of lading is still relatively unknown

Consignor

Emblem of National Association

FBL

NEGOTIABLE FIATA
COMBINED TRANSPORT
BILL OF LADING

issued subject to ICC Uniform Rules for a Combined Transport Document (ICC publication 298).

Consigned to order of

Notify address

	Place of receipt
Ocean vessel	Port of loading
Port of discharge	Place of delivery

Marks and numbers	Number and kind of packages	Description of goods	Gross weight	Measurement

specimen

according to the declaration of the consignor

The goods and instructions are accepted and dealt with subject to the Standard Conditions printed overleaf.

Taken in charge in apparent good order and condition, unless otherwise noted herein, at the place of receipt for transport and delivery as mentioned above.

One of these Combined Transport Bills of Lading must be surrendered duly endorsed in exchange for the goods. In Witness whereof the original Combined Transport Bills of Lading all of this tenor and date have been signed in the number stated below, one of which being accomplished the other(s) to be void.

Freight amount	Freight payable at	Place and date of issue
Cargo Insurance through the undersigned ☐ not covered ☐ Covered according to attached Policy	Number of Original FBL's	Stamp and signature
For delivery of goods please apply to:		

Figure 6.8 *A negotiable FIATA combined transport bill of lading*

Consignor

FBL

Customs Reference/Status | FBL No | GB

Shipper's Reference

Forwarder's Reference

Consignee (or order)

Registered No 0087

NEGOTIABLE FIATA COMBINED TRANSPORT BILL OF LADING

ICC

issued subject to ICC Uniform Rules for a Combined Transport Document (ICC publication 298)

FIATA FBL Licence No. 1008

Notify Address

MOONBRIDGE

MOONBRIDGE SHIPPERS LTD

Balfour House 390/398 High Road, Ilford, Essex IG1 1UH ENGLAND
Telephone: 01-478 6911 Telex 897406

Ocean Vessel	Port of Loading	Place of Receipt
Port of Discharge	Final Destination (If on-carriage)	Place of Delivery

Marks and Numbers	Number and Kind of Packages	Description of Goods	Gross Weight (Kilos)	Measurement (M^3)

SPECIMEN ONLY

Container/Trailer Number

Seal Number

Total Packages

according to the declaration of the consignor

Text authorised by FIATA. Copyright Reserved FIATA/Zurich-Switzerland 8-87

2-88

The goods and instructions are accepted and dealt with subject to the Standard Conditions printed overleaf.

Taken in charge in apparent good order and condition, unless otherwise noted herein, at the place of receipt for transport and delivery as mentioned above.

One of these Combined Transport Bills of Lading must be surrendered duly endorsed in exchange for the goods. In Witness whereof the original Combined Transport Bills of Lading all of this tenor and date have been signed in the number stated below, one of which being accomplished the other(s) to be void.

Freight Amount	Freight Payable at	Place and date of issue, Stamp and signature
Cargo Insurance through the undersigned ☐ Not covered ☐ Covered according to attached Policy	Number of Original FBL's	LONDON
For delivery of goods please apply to		SPECIMEN ONLY For & on behalf of Moonbridge Shippers Limited

SYSTEMFORMS LTD 01-505 6125

Figure 6.9 *A personalised FIATA combined transport bill of lading*

and under-used for world trade, but its usage is likely to increase as its advantages become more widely appreciated. Well established freight forwarders will often personalise the FIATA bill of lading (see Figure 6.9), so that their name and address appear prominently on the actual bill. This practice helps the companies to market their services, and customers know that if the bill of lading has the FIATA cachet they are dealing with a reliable freight forwarder.

Freight forwarder's bill of lading. Freight forwarders who provide NVOCC consolidation services (see Chapter 5) often issue their own bill of lading, frequently referred to as a house bill or groupage bill. The reason is that they want to give their services a marketing personality. Shipping lines will issue only one bill of lading for the whole container and the forwarder then issues an individual bill for every shipment.

In appearance an NVOCC bill of lading looks no different from the FIATA bill and, if the freight forwarder has a good reputation and works with first-class agents around the world, there should be no difficulties. However, the provider of an NVOCC service relies on the shipping lines for the performance of the service, and many people argue that the freight forwarder is issuing a bill of lading which lacks meaning.

As a precaution, shippers should ask the NVOCC operator about insurance cover and liability in the case of cargo loss or damage, and again the reputable freight forwarder will have excellent arrangements. Yet the NVOCC bill of lading does not have the legal strength or recognition of the ocean bill or the FIATA bill. If a letter of credit demands an ocean bill as one of its conditions, the NVOCC bill will in most cases be rejected by the banks. The FIATA bill is, however, acceptable in these circumstances. Certain countries of the world also refuse to recognise the validity of an NVOCC bill.

Regular and financially reliable customers overseas will be supplied on an 'open account' basis which means that the exporter trusts that payment will be made in accordance with agreed conditions. 'Open account' trading can only exist when there is confidence between the buyer and seller. Shipments which are being sent regularly on 'open account', for which the bill of lading is not used as a part of the financial transaction, can be covered by the NVOCC bill of lading. For more complicated movements, careful checking should precede any decision to accept an NVOCC bill.

Problems with bills of lading
There are hundreds of legal precedents which have framed custom and practice regarding bills of lading. All these cases arose, naturally enough, when something went wrong and the dispute ended up in the courts. Those who require more details of the legal minefield surrounding bills of lading

should read *Export Trade: Law and Practice of International Trade* by Clive M Schmitthoff (published by Stevens & Sons, 1986).

It is not uncommon to have a bill of lading claused, and the clause may draw attention to some damage to the goods which the shipping line has noticed. Depending on the extent of the damage and the way the transaction is being financed, a claused bill may be rejected by a bank. A 'stale' bill is one which reaches the port of destination after the goods have arrived, and this again can lead to problems.

One of the commonest problems with bills of lading is their loss, often in the postal system. This can be avoided if the shipping line issues two or three originals, and one original bill is held by the shipper as an insurance policy in the event of loss. In view of the value of the bill of lading, it is also worthwhile sending it by registered post at all times so some degree of control is possible.

If an original bill of lading is irretrievably lost, the shipping line will only issue a duplicate if they are given a letter of indemnity by the consignee which will cover their potential liability in case anyone ever presents the original bill in the future.

Air waybill
The air waybill (see Figure 6.10), often abbreviated to AWB, is used for all air freight and acts as the consignment note. Unlike the bill of lading the air waybill is not a document of title. The basic air waybill is a 12-part document with each page fulfilling a different purpose, even though for many jobs not all 12 copies are required.

The air waybill can be completed by the airline, although it is normally the air freight forwarder who will establish the document. The air waybill is used in all communications regarding the shipment as well as on other forms used for customs formalities. The number in the top right-hand corner is unique and is used to identify the goods at all stages of their journey as well as when they are collected by the consignee. It is important to let your customer have the air waybill number as soon as possible.

The air waybill provides the shipper with proof of receipt for the goods, and other copies of the waybill accompany the consignment. The waybill is also used as an accounting document with charges added as the goods move through various stages of their journey. Even if goods are transferred from one airline to another to complete the journey, the original waybill can still be used. The waybill is a standardised document which is used by IATA and non-IATA airlines alike. IATA operates a worldwide account system in which almost all airlines participate even if they are not full members of IATA.

Completing an air waybill is relatively easy and most of the information

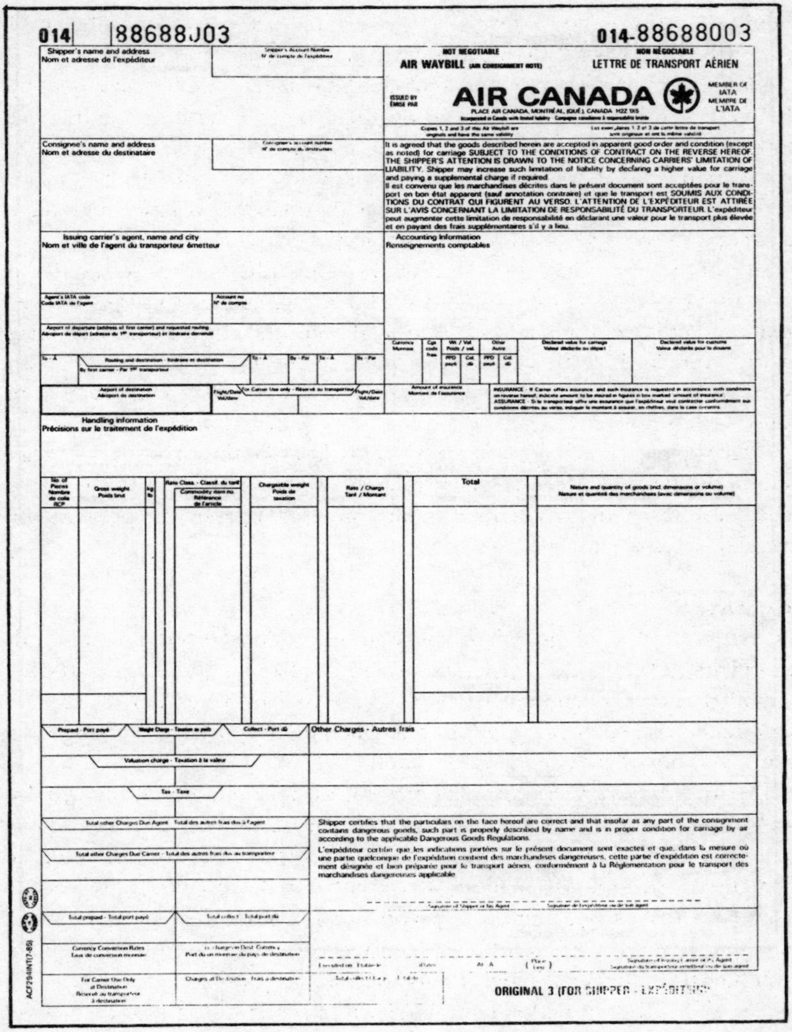

014 | 88688J03

014-88688003

Shipper's name and address
Nom et adresse de l'expéditeur

Shipper's Account Number
Nº de compte de l'expéditeur

NOT NEGOTIABLE
AIR WAYBILL (AIR CONSIGNMENT NOTE)

NON NÉGOCIABLE
LETTRE DE TRANSPORT AÉRIEN

ISSUED BY
ÉMISE PAR

AIR CANADA
PLACE AIR CANADA, MONTRÉAL (QUÉ.), CANADA H2Z 1X5

MEMBER OF IATA
MEMBRE DE L'IATA

Consignee's name and address
Nom et adresse du destinataire

It is agreed that the goods described herein are accepted in apparent good order and condition (except as noted) for carriage SUBJECT TO THE CONDITIONS OF CONTRACT ON THE REVERSE HEREOF. THE SHIPPER'S ATTENTION IS DRAWN TO THE NOTICE CONCERNING CARRIERS' LIMITATION OF LIABILITY. Shipper may increase such limitation of liability by declaring a higher value for carriage and paying a supplemental charge if required.

Il est convenu que les marchandises décrites dans le présent document sont acceptées pour le transport en bon état apparent (sauf annotation contraire) et que le transport est SOUMIS AUX CONDITIONS DU CONTRAT QUI FIGURENT AU VERSO. L'ATTENTION DE L'EXPÉDITEUR EST ATTIRÉE SUR L'AVIS CONCERNANT LA LIMITATION DE RESPONSABILITÉ DU TRANSPORTEUR. L'expéditeur peut augmenter cette limitation de responsabilité en déclarant une valeur pour le transport plus élevée et en payant des frais supplémentaires s'il y a lieu.

Issuing carrier's agent, name and city
Nom et ville de l'agent du transporteur émetteur

Accounting Information
Renseignements comptables

Agent's IATA code
Code IATA de l'agent

Account no
Nº de compte

Airport of departure (address of first carrier) and requested routing
Aéroport de départ (adresse du 1er transporteur) et itinéraire demandé

To - À | Routing and destination - Itinéraire et destination | By first carrier - Par 1er transporteur | To - À | By - Par | To - À | By - Par

Currency / Monnaie | Cgs code | Wt / Val Poids / val. PPD payé Coll dû | Other Autre PPD payé Coll dû | Declared value for carriage / Valeur déclarée au départ | Declared value for customs / Valeur déclarée pour la douane

Airport of destination
Aéroport de destination

Flight/Date Vol/date | For Carrier Use only - Réservé au transporteur | Flight/Date Vol/date

Amount of insurance
Montant de l'assurance

Handling information
Précisions sur le traitement de l'expédition

No. of Pieces / Nombre de colis RCP | Gross weight / Poids brut | kg lb | Rate Class - Classif. du tarif / Commodity item no. Référence de l'article | Chargeable weight / Poids de taxation | Rate / Charge Tarif / Montant | Total | Nature and quantity of goods (incl. dimensions or volume) / Nature et quantité des marchandises (avec dimensions ou volume)

Prepaid - Port payé | Weight Charge - Taxation au poids | Collect - Port dû

Other Charges - Autres frais

Valuation charge - Taxation à la valeur

Tax - Taxe

Total other Charges Due Agent - Total des autres frais dus à l'agent

Total other Charges Due Carrier - Total des autres frais dus au transporteur

Shipper certifies that the particulars on the face hereof are correct and that insofar as any part of the consignment contains dangerous goods, such part is properly described by name and is in proper condition for carriage by air according to the applicable Dangerous Goods Regulations.

L'expéditeur certifie que les indications portées sur le présent document sont exactes et que, dans la mesure où une partie quelconque de l'expédition contient des marchandises dangereuses, cette partie d'expédition est correctement désignée et bien préparée pour le transport aérien, conformément à la Réglementation pour le transport des marchandises dangereuses applicable.

Signature of Shipper or his Agent — Signature de l'expéditeur ou de son agent

Total prepaid - Total port payé | Total collect - Total port dû

Currency Conversion Rates
Taux de conversion monnaie

Executed on / Établie le (Date) At / À (Place / Lieu)

Signature of Issuing Carrier or its Agent

For Carrier Use Only at Destination
Réservé au transporteur à destination

Charges at Destination - Frais à destination

ORIGINAL 3 (FOR SHIPPER - EXPÉDITEUR)

ACF294INT(7-85)

Figure 6.10 *An airline air waybill*

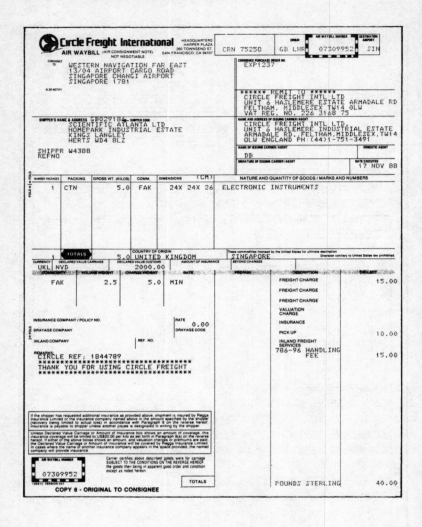

Figure 6.11 *A house air waybill*

requirements are self-evident. It is the responsibility of the air freight forwarder to ensure accuracy; any mistakes can, as with all other documents, create problems.

House air waybill
A growing trend in air freight is for freight forwarders to issue their own house air waybills (see Figure 6.11), abbreviated to HAWB. These are similar to the air waybills issued by the airlines. The air freight forwarder consolidates several shipments under one master air waybill, known as an MAWB, and then issues individual air waybills to customers.

When goods are being sent by air freight under a letter of credit, the letter of credit will stipulate certain information which must be included on the waybill. As long as the conditions of the letter of credit are strictly followed, the air waybill can be submitted to the bank with all the other documents. The only practical drawback is that air freight operates far more quickly than the banking system and, by the time the sheaf of documents has been lodged with the UK bank, the goods will already be at their destination. Therefore, if payment is required before the goods are delivered, it is more sensible to instruct your freight forwarder to despatch the goods on a cash on delivery basis. There will be a modest handling charge for this service, but at least the shipment will not be delayed and incur unnecessary storage costs.

Certificate of shipment
Exporters will frequently come across a certificate of shipment (see Figure 6.12) which is a document issued by a freight forwarder confirming that goods have been despatched overseas. As well as a description of the goods, the certificate of shipment contains other details such as the trailer or container number and the port of loading and discharge.

For goods moving across to another part of Europe on a groupage service, the freight forwarder automatically issues the shipper with a certificate of shipment unless any other document has been specifically requested.

Customs forms: Single Administrative Document

The Single Administrative Document (SAD) was introduced in January 1988 and replaced many of the existing customs forms. The SAD (see Figure 6.13) is used throughout the European Community and, apart from language differences, all member states of the EC use the same form. The technical name for the SAD in the UK is the C88 – this number appears in the bottom left-hand corner of the document.

The SAD is an eight-part document which in theory should accompany

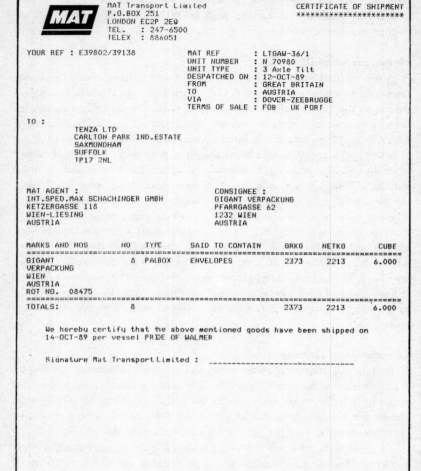

Figure 6.12 *A certificate of shipment*

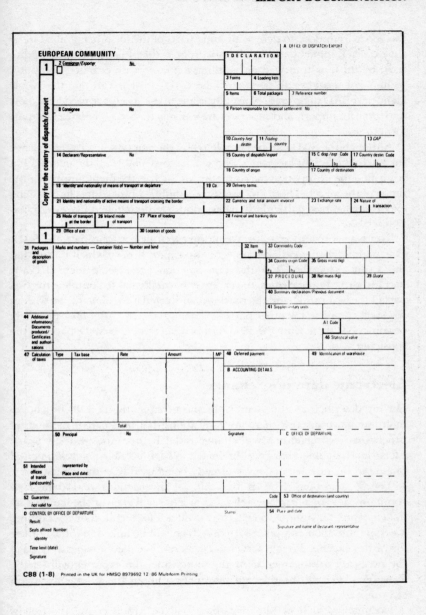

Figure 6.13 *The Single Adminstrative Document*

the goods from door to door with some parts of the form being filled in by the exporter, some by the freight forwarder at the time of export and other parts by the freight forwarder handling the import. In practice, computer technology has already overtaken the SAD, so it is rare for the whole eight-part SAD to be used. Normally, some of the sheets are used for export and some for import, and exporters are unlikely to see a complete eight-part form in use.

Although the SAD can be completed by the shipper, it is easier to leave the job to the freight forwarder who will have available all the information regarding the transport of the consignment, such as the flight number or the name of the vessel. There are also some simplified procedures for fulfilling export formalities, particularly when goods are despatched in a consolidation service.

There are certain occasions when the exporter has to initiate the SAD. One such is when goods are subject to an export licence which means that they cannot leave the UK without the sanction of the Department of Trade and Industry. In these cases, the exporter normally has to complete the first part of the SAD and hand the partially completed form on to the forwarder who will complete the other parts in the normal way. After checking, UK customs will then send the first stamped sheet of the SAD back to the consignor.

Electronic data interchange

Having described at some length the most frequently used documents in international transport, there are indications that the current methods of processing documentation will change radically over the next few years. Electronic data interchange, abbreviated to EDI, is still in a developmental phase but the new technology is already being used by some companies.

The idea behind EDI is that all the instructions and data now communicated by telephone, telex, fax or letter will in future be handled by linked computer systems. So exporters will ask for a collection by tapping messages into their computer systems which will be linked to those of their forwarding agents. Freight forwarders will retrieve the messages and make the necessary arrangements. At the same time, the exporter will let the forwarder have all the relevant information about the shipments, again electronically.

Documents, such as bills of lading, will be produced by the freight forwarder who, again through the computer, will ensure that original bills and copies are printed out on the exporter's system. Simultaneously, copy bills of lading will be available to the bank and agents overseas. Many experts argue that the printed documents will not actually be required, as all the necessary information about a consignment can be accessed from a screen.

The widespread introduction of EDI could save shippers a great deal of time. At the moment, it is estimated that documentation costs amount to an average 7 per cent of any shipment. In addition, EDI has the capacity to minimise errors, although this assumes that correct information is input in the first place. The British International Freight Association (BIFA) has taken a leading role in the introduction of EDI within the freight forwarding industry by establishing, together with the company Export Network, the Freight Forwarder's Network. This system allows freight forwarders and their customers access to a common user EDI network at a reasonable cost. Larger freight forwarders are probably more likely to join the EDI network in their own right, but the BIFA initiative means that companies of all sizes have the potential benefits of the latest EDI developments. Similarly, IBM United Kingdom provides a system, illustrated in Figure 6.14, which links participating companies around the world through the IBM information network.

The drawback of EDI is that no common standards have been adopted. This means that shippers may need several terminals if they are dealing with a variety of shipping lines, airlines, hauliers and freight forwarders. Most exporters deal with more than one freight forwarder in the sensible belief

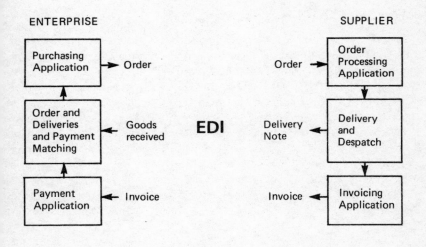

Source: IBM United Kingdom Limited

Figure 6.14 *An example of an EDI system – the IBM information network*

that some companies specialise in certain areas, and shippers will not want their choice restricted by the limitations of modern technology. Under the auspices of the United Nations, an attempt has been made to establish international standards based on Edifact, which is the name for one of the many EDI systems available. Edifact is the official standard of the EC and is also gaining acceptance in North America.

EDI systems are being introduced in several industries – particularly retailing and motor manufacturing. Therefore, a company which intends to embrace EDI for its transport requirements must also consider the EDI standards of its own industry. The challenge for the transport industry is to try to agree on a standard worldwide EDI system, in which case the concept of EDI will become more attractive to large and small shippers alike.

Despite the technological attractions of EDI, many small exporters will still rely on the traditional methods of communication – the telephone, the postal system and the typewriter. This means that freight forwarders will in future be dealing with two distinct groups of customer: those linked to an EDI network and those who have decided to remain loyal to their tried and tested shipping systems. In the meantime, exporters should try to keep abreast of developments and make use of any opportunities which arise.

Chapter 7

Import Documentation

Introduction

Many of the forms required for importing goods are exactly the same as those for exporting. These include invoices, packing lists, the certificate of origin, the CMR form, bill of lading and air waybill. Importers will generally need to ensure that the freight forwarder completing UK import formalities has all the necessary paperwork.

For imports, it is not the importer who is responsible for creating the documents, and so his role is restricted to ensuring that the documentation is correct and supplied in good time. In most cases invoices and other documents will arrive with the goods as, contrary to UK practice, countries abroad do not allow goods to be despatched without the correct documents already having been prepared.

Importers will always require invoices. For goods coming into the UK by sea, the importer will often receive the original bill of lading from the overseas supplier, and it is essential that this document is passed on to the freight forwarder so that customs formalities can be completed. To avoid duplication, none of the documents described in Chapter 6 will be included in this chapter, which will concentrate on the documentation relevant to importing only.

Every country controls import traffic more strictly than export traffic. The reason for this is historical as importing has traditionally been regarded as slightly unpatriotic, although with the creation of the EC and the widening consumer demand for more varied and exotic goods this view attracts less support.

Imports are also important because the government obtains considerable revenue from imports – from duty and, above all in the UK, from VAT. Although duty on imports from other members of the EC and EFTA countries is almost non-existent, it is still payable on a wide range of products which come from other parts of the world. Under the influence of the General Agreement on Tariffs and Trade (GATT), duty on all products has come down. UK importers should rarely be troubled by a rate of duty in excess of about 7 per cent and most items attract duty at a far lower rate.

VAT is of greater significance as it is imputed at the standard rate (currently 15 per cent) on all items subject to VAT. There are exemptions, such as food, but in general most importers will have to pay VAT on everything they import into the UK.

Customs forms: Single Administrative Document

The Single Administrative Document (SAD) (see Figure 6.13 on page 87) is used for both import and export formalities. As previously explained, it is more likely that the SAD is used in its component parts, and for importing goods it is sheets 6, 7 and 8 of the eight-part document which are used. In fact, even this is quite rare, as most main ports and airports in the UK are linked to the Direct Trader Input system. This is a computerised system for customs clearance which enables freight forwarders to prepare and enter the consignment through a computer system which links the forwarder with HM Customs.

Unless customs call the goods for a physical examination (often referred to as a Route 3 clearance) or there is some other query, the whole clearance procedure is carried out via the Direct Trader Input system. This is far quicker than completing the SAD form manually, although all the information required on the form is still needed to complete the Direct Trader Input entry. A further advantage of the system is that duty and VAT liability are automatically calculated on the basis of the data punched in by the entry clerk.

Import licences

All imports require a licence which is granted by the Department of Trade and Industry (DTI). The exceptions to this rule are certain food products and personal effects for people coming to live in the UK.

The requirement for an import licence may seem surprising, as in practice most importers rarely, if ever, see one. The reason is that the DTI issues Open General Licences which cover the vast majority of goods. These Open General Licences are held by the DTI and allow an unspecified amount of each product into the country, which means that importers do not have to obtain a specific licence for every consignment. The government has the reserve power to withdraw the Open General Licence at any time if it wants to limit the amount of a particular product coming into the UK. This reserve power is now constrained in the light of the treaty obligations arising from membership of the EC.

Some goods are still subject to import licensing and, if goods fall into this category, application for a licence should be made by the importer before the goods arrive in the UK. If the licence is not available, the consignment will be held up in customs and the importer faced with the inevitable high storage charges. The types of product which are subject to licence are either controlled goods, such as arms or drugs, or sensitive commodities, such as textiles. In many cases, the requirement for an import licence applies only because the government wants to maintain a stricter quantifiable control of the total amount of the product being brought into the country. For other goods, the import licence acts as a strict control and the government wants to limit the total quantity of goods allowed into the UK.

Methods of customs clearance – DEPS

The Direct Trader Input system is linked to another computer, the Departmental Entry Processing System (DEPS), and feeds information into it. At the major airports of Gatwick, Heathrow and Manchester, the link with DEPS is through a different system called ACP 90. The method of entering goods is slightly different but the way the system operates is similar to Direct Trader Input. Similar systems which link all the local freight forwarders to DEPS have been installed at major import locations including Felixstowe, Southampton and the Port of London. All the systems are registered under different names but, from the importer's point of view, the result is the same – a direct link between the clearing agents and DEPS. There is a plan to replace all these systems with CHIEF (Customs Handling of Import and Export Freight) but it is not expected to be available before 1991 or even later. Importers do not have to understand the detailed workings of these systems as they will be employing a freight forwarder whose responsibility is to handle the import of the consignment. Nevertheless, as some of these terms are constantly mentioned, it is just as well to have an understanding of how the system operates.

Local Import Clearance

The tradition in the UK has been for customs clearance procedures to be carried out at the port of entry. This is a result of the UK being an island and, before the arrival of air freight, all goods came into the country by sea. Still today, most goods which arrive by sea or by truck are cleared at the port of arrival.

The system on the Continent is quite different. Most borders are land frontiers, and goods are subject to few checks at the border. The clearance formalities are usually carried out in the main inland commercial centres where there are large depots and sheds under customs control. In addition, many Continental freight forwarders have the authority to clear goods at their own warehouse, subject to the periodic checking of a customs official.

The UK customs authorities are now trying to draw more customs clearance work inland. This strategy prompted the introduction in 1989, on an experimental basis, of Local Import Clearance (LIC). Under the LIC scheme, HM Customs have granted a small number of freight forwarders the right to clear goods at their own premises. The forwarders are linked to the Direct Trader Input system so customs entries are completed electronically. If customs decide that they want to examine a consignment, an official will visit the forwarder's premises, and, in the meantime, the goods will not be released.

The aim behind the LIC scheme is to speed up customs clearance. Entries can be prepared and logged into the Direct Trader Input system before the arrival of the trailer so that only consignments under query are delayed. At the moment, the LIC scheme applies only to goods from the EC, and this restricts its appeal mainly to freight forwarders who operate trailer groupage services. It is expected, however, that the LIC scheme will eventually be extended to cover non-EC traffic. The freight forwarders who have obtained the LIC authorisation claim that they can provide significant reductions in total transit times. For small businesses, an LIC licensed freight forwarder, such as Sea Route Ferry of Eastleigh, is certainly worth considering if delays in customs clearance are already being experienced. While HM Customs have tried to transfer some of the clearance work inland, a new scheme which speeds up import formalities at ports and airports. has also been introduced.

Fast Lane

The Fast Lane system for customs clearance was introduced in September 1989. Like LIC, Fast Lane applies only to goods from the EC, so it has more relevance to international hauliers and groupage operators than to air freight forwarders or deep-sea specialists.

The idea behind Fast Lane is to speed up customs clearance in advance of the creation of the Single Market (see Chapter 13). Under a special system, the freight forwarder at the port can enter the details of the goods while the trailer is still on the ferry and, unless there is a query, the Direct Trader Input system will authorise an immediate clearance. For the trailer operator, this means that the vehicle should not remain at the port for more than about half an hour after the arrival of the ferry. Most agents at the major Ro-Ro ports of Dover, Felixstowe, Hull and Poole are using the Fast Lane facility so, unless there are any specific problems, the time taken for UK customs clearance is now being reduced to a minimum.

The tariff

On every SAD, there is a box which requires the commodity code for the particular consignment to be inserted. The commodity code is usually a nine- or eleven-digit number which relates to a particular consignment. All these numbers come from the customs tariff.

At the beginning of 1988, the UK along with the other members of the EC switched to a tariff which is based on the Harmonised System (HS). The new HS was developed after many years of discussion and HS is used by about 85 per cent of the world's trading nations.

The UK tariff consists of three volumes and can be purchased for about £100. The second volume is the most important one for traders; 97 chapters list a whole range of products. Importers can study Volume 2 and will usually find a description of the goods they are importing. Alongside the description is the commodity code, and it is this commodity code which appears on the SAD and determines the rate of duty payable and the rate of VAT – zero or standard rated.

Companies which import from the EC require a nine-digit commodity code whereas imports from the rest of the world require an eleven-digit classification. This is a general rule and there are exceptions, particularly with agricultural products. However, for most imports of manufactured goods, the nine- and eleven-digit rule is valid. Exporters also need the correct commodity code, but the requirement for all export traffic is nine digits only, irrespective of the destination.

The responsibility for supplying the correct commodity code to HM Customs lies with the importer and, if there is an incorrect classification, any fines levied are the responsibility of the importer and not the freight forwarder. In practical terms, this does not mean that every small importer has to go out and buy a copy of the tariff; it is an expensive document which would be used infrequently. Freight forwarders have the most recent tariff available, and they have a great deal of experience in advising importers on the appropriate tariff code. Consultation with an efficient freight forwarder will soon lead to a correct classification and, as most firms tend to import the same type of goods, forwarders will store the relevant commodity codes in their customer database for subsequent shipments.

VAT

Import procedures involve the payment of VAT. Regular importers of a sufficiently high financial standing should apply for a deferment account number from HM Customs. A deferment number (often referred to as a DAN) is a unique five-digit number which, with proper authorisation, can be given to the freight forwarder to include in the appropriate part of the customs entry. The forwarder uses this number and HM Customs will automatically charge all the VAT due to the importer's deferment. Around the middle of every month, the importer receives a statement listing all the VAT payable for imports and must then settle the account.

HM Customs lays down certain financial criteria, including a guarantee, for obtaining a deferment. The deferment is also set at a predetermined amount and, once this has been reached each month, the importer will have to apply for a higher limit in the future, and in the meantime settle the excess amount by banker's draft or cash.

The alternative to a deferment is paying the VAT due when goods are imported. Freight forwarders are unlikely to extend credit for VAT, so will not release shipments until they have received a banker's draft. Raising and delivering the draft can take time – goods may be delayed unless payment arrangements have been made before the goods arrive.

The decision on whether to apply for a deferment depends on the number of import shipments expected as well as the cash flow implications. Using a deferment allows the importer about six weeks' credit, but this has to be weighed against the financial cost of a guarantee. The question of how VAT is to be paid should be considered when first looking into the possibility of importing goods.

Once the goods have been imported, the freight forwarder will send the VAT certificate to the importer. This is an important document as it is used as evidence of VAT paid on imports, and the amounts are offset against the other amounts due from the importer. The system of distribution for these VAT certificates is rather bureaucratic; the form originates with HM Customs who send it to the freight forwarder who prepared the customs entry, and the forwarder sends it on. There are, therefore, plenty of opportunities for the form to be delayed or mislaid, and it is important for the small importer to keep track of every VAT certificate. No other document is accepted by HM Customs as proof of payment. It would be far easier for HM Customs to send the VAT certificates direct to importers but this modest change has so far proved elusive.

Chapter 8
Special Despatches

Introduction

Some goods require special handling, perhaps because they are delicate or because they pose a potential danger. Some types of special despatches can be sent together with other goods but the documentary requirements are different. This is the case with exhibition goods and hazardous cargo.

Great care must be taken with special despatches. Inadequate or incorrect documentation may delay the goods or the importer may be obliged to pay unnecessary customs duties. Damage can occur in transit and may happen, for example, when an exporter, used to despatching heavy machinery, sends his customers some delicate artefacts as Christmas presents. If the packing specifications are not altered for the gifts, disaster may well follow.

The demand for special shipments is a permanent feature of commercial life, and a brief survey of the common categories of such shipments is outlined in this chapter.

Antiques and fine arts

The UK is an international centre for the art and antique world, and there is a continuous flow of pictures, furniture and other valuables in and out of the country. People come from all over the world to attend auctions in the UK, and they then need their purchases shipped home. The shipment of fine arts is a specialised activity, and there are freight forwarders who handle this type of business. All aspects of the transport will cost substantially more than sending general cargo, but a great deal more care and effort is involved.

The correct packing of antiques is important. Furniture and pictures have to be packed in strong, wooden cases. Timber is expensive and the packing cost can often be more expensive than the freight. For deep-sea shipments, wooden packing is essential, but for air freight or trailer movement, it may be possible to protect the package with corrugated board, thick paper and blankets. This will suffice as long as the freight agent does not load the Chippendale table alongside some steel bars. This is not a fanciful suggestion, as depots around the world are littered with pieces of

97

smashed furniture and fragments of broken china and glass.

Paying a cheap price for the transport of antique items will almost inevitably lead to damage. Works of art do not deserve rough treatment.

Books and printed matter

UK publishers export well over 30 per cent of their annual production, and there is also a healthy import of books, mainly from the USA. In addition, magazines and newspapers are moving around the world every day, and the explosion of the printed word has also led to the despatch of brochures to customers overseas. Just to complicate the picture, a great deal of magazine printing takes place abroad.

The largest shipper of printed matter is the Post Office which has a range of specialised services to meet the requirements of the book trade. The Post Office will despatch books and magazines by road, sea and air, offering discounts for printed matter. For small quantities of goods, the Post Office is highly competitive and cheaper than any other carrier, mainly because its price structure has low minimum rates.

The price structure of the Post Office works against itself for larger shipments, and several freight forwarders have developed specialised services aimed specifically at the book trade. Rates are more competitive and the service is more flexible. The forwarders can also provide a far tighter control of the consignment which, in view of the volume of their traffic, is quite impossible for the Post Office. These specialised forwarders will provide a full door-to-door service including the re-mailing of individual packages. This type of service is particularly important for books and magazines going to the USA or the Continent. The first part of the movement is handled as a bulk shipment and, once in the country of destination, the shipments are split up and fed into the domestic postal network or delivered by a dedicated delivery company.

Computer hardware and spares

The international movement of computers is a fast-growing business and there are several companies which have established a reputation in this field. Computers are very delicate and vibration during transit can cause extensive damage. The packing of computers is thus important and all moving parts should, as far as possible, be immobilised.

Vehicles for the transport of computers are carefully designed. The lorries are well sprung and have additional air suspension. The interiors are padded and strapping inside the trailers enables the computers to be firmly tied down.

If all proper precautions are taken, there will be no harmful movement. At a price, delivery can be effected throughout Europe, although the carrier must be instructed to avoid transhipment of the goods at any stage. For overseas destinations, air freight is the best solution.

The value of computers makes it essential for the exporter to supervise the shipment at all times. Engineers should organise the loading into the lorry or aircraft and arrange to monitor the shipment until it is delivered. The transport of computers is expensive, although the value of the cargo should prevent any temptation to cut corners.

High-technology products provide a significant volume of air freight cargo, and the transport of spare parts for these items is much easier. Speed is always important, so the advice is to choose the quickest service whether by air, land or sea. Again, several freight forwarders specialise in high-technology traffic. Often the customs clearance of these products is more of a headache than the physical movement.

Dangerous goods

The transport of dangerous goods needs to be undertaken with particular care, as any accidents during transport can lead to appalling injuries or death. The range of goods classified as dangerous is extremely wide, although the largest single category consists of chemicals. Yet for transport purposes, many products normally considered quite harmless are classified as hazardous. Thus, whisky and other spirits are considered hazardous if they are packed in containers with a capacity of more than five litres. Nail varnish and shampoo also become hazardous commodities for transport purposes. These products are liable to ignite or give off a vapour which can damage other cargoes in certain circumstances. Other chemicals, notably acids, are corrosive.

Shippers of dangerous goods must always declare them before despatch. Failure to declare hazardous products is an offence and enforcement regulations are being tightened up all the time. Apart from risking prosecution, shippers who do not declare hazardous goods are wilfully endangering innocent people and the environment. Some companies are reluctant to declare hazardous goods, either because they are ignorant of the regulations or because they want to avoid paying the higher freight charges. Handling hazardous goods is more expensive for carriers, so in most cases a hazardous surcharge justifiably applies.

With prior warning, dangerous chemicals will be accepted for shipment by air, road and sea, although each mode of transport has different regulations. Thus, goods which are being taken by truck and then by air will have to comply with the rules governing both road and air shipments.

The first step for the manufacturer is to provide full details of the shipment to the freight forwarder who will be able to provide information about the special procedures to be adopted. These rules relate to the packaging and clear labelling of the cargo as well as any restrictions regarding transport. The onus is on the shipper to provide all the necessary information, and this obligation is enshrined in the Conveyance, Packaging and Labelling Regulations (CPR). The most important part of the CPR is the marking of hazardous goods as hazardous. Any failure on the part of the shipper to notify the transport operator about the nature of a hazard could lead to prosecution under the Health and Safety at Work Act.

Dangerous goods by air

The regulations governing the movement of dangerous goods by air are stricter than those applied to other methods of transport. The reasons for these strict controls are logical enough – first, the presence of passengers in the same aircraft, and second, the additional risk of goods being affected by changes in air pressure. The carriage of dangerous goods is one of the advantages of using cargo-only aircraft. There are certain commodities which can be shipped in cargo-only aircraft but cannot be carried on passenger flights.

Everyone involved in the shipping of dangerous goods must comply with the regulations laid down by the International Civil Aviation Organisation (ICAO) and IATA. The rules are policed in the UK by the Civil Aviation Authority (CAA). Every IATA registered air freight forwarder has to ensure that a proportion of their staff undergoes periodic training and re-validation courses in the carriage of dangerous goods. The course content itself is verified and licensed by the CAA.

Every chemical is classified according to a class number between one and nine. Class 1 consists of explosives, and Class 9 consists of miscellaneous dangerous goods. Most of the classes also have subdivisions, and it is the responsibility of the shipper to advise the air freight forwarder of the class number. The ICAO regulations provide details of the requirements for packing, labelling, documentation and transport. All the regulations regarding the handling and transport of dangerous goods are legally binding.

The most important form which the shipper has to complete is the shipper's declaration and from this the air freight forwarder will complete the airway bill.

Dangerous goods by sea

The regulations for the movement of dangerous goods by sea are established by the International Maritime Consultative Organisation (IMCO) which is a United Nations sponsored organisation. IMCO has established the International Maritime Dangerous Goods Code (the IMDG Code) which has largely been included in UK law through the Merchant Shipping (Dangerous Goods) Regulations 1981. These regulations apply once the container is loaded on to a vessel, and also between the loading point and the port.

Companies which regularly send hazardous goods abroad should buy the *IMCO Blue Book* which lists the regulations for every commodity. The book also includes emergency procedures. The regulations for sea transport are legally binding and must be followed. Products which are classified in the higher class numbers have often only to be notified to the shipping line to be accepted. The line will then ensure that the container is stowed in a particular part of the ship, and that no substances likely to be affected are stowed in the immediate vicinity.

To arrange shipment, the manufacturer must give full details of the products to the freight forwarder who can advise on packaging, labelling and documentation requirements. The forwarder will liaise with the shipping line, and normally make a special application – often called a special stowage order. The shipping line then advises the forwarder when the goods can be accepted. Rules governing the segregation of different types of hazardous cargo are laid down in the IMDG Code, and these rules must be obeyed. The forwarder will arrange to deliver the goods to the quay and complete a dangerous goods note (see Figure 8.1).

Full container load and less than container load dangerous cargo can be shipped, although it is sometimes more difficult to send smaller quantities. Non-Vessel Owning Common Carrier (NVOCC) operators have to be careful not to load hazardous goods together with an incompatible cargo. For instance, some chemicals may give off a vapour which can ruin foodstuffs. In addition, one hazardous shipment may be acceptable in a container, but the freight forwarder may frequently find himself with two or three to send in the same unit. These are some of the problems that have to be overcome but, with patience and scrupulous attention to detail, most types of hazardous goods can be shipped.

Dangerous goods by road

The movement of hazardous goods by road in Europe is governed by the IMDG Code and the Accord Dangereux Routier (ADR). Although usually referred to as ADR, the English translation is the International Carriage of Dangerous Goods. Several hauliers specialise in the carriage of dangerous goods and both their drivers and their office staff are familiar with the regulations.

A further complication for Ro-Ro traffic is that, when the trailer is on the

DG DANGEROUS GOODS DECLARATION, SHIPPING NOTE & CONTAINER/VEHICLE PACKING CERTIFICATE © SITPRO 1985

DANGEROUS GOODS NOTE

Special Information is required for (a) Dangerous Goods in Limited Quantities (b) Radioactive Substances (class 7) (c) Tank Containers and (d) in certain circumstances a weathering certificate is required

SHADED AREAS NEED NOT BE SHIPPER COMPLETED FOR SHORT SEA, RO, RO, RAIL.

| Exporter | | 1 | Veh Bkg. Ref. | 2 | Customs Reference/Status | 3 |

Exporter's Reference 4

Export Freight Forwarder / Port Charges Payable by * 5 | Fwdr's Ref. 6 | SS Co Bkg No. 7

Consignee 8A | Other (Name & Address)

Name of Shipping Line or CTO 8 | Port Account No.

Freight Forwarder 9 | For Use of Receiving Authority Only

Receiving Date(s) | Berth/Dock/Containerbase etc. 10

Consecutive no. or DG reference allocated by shipping line or C.T.O. (if any) 10A

Vessel | Port of Loading 11 | TO THE RECEIVING AUTHORITY Please receive for shipment the goods described below subject to your published regulations & conditions (including those as to liability)

Port of Discharge | Destination Depot 12 | Name of Receiving Authority 13

Marks & Numbers; No. & Kind of Packages. Description of goods. † INDICATE: HAZARD CLASS, UN NUMBER, FLASHPOINT °C. 14 | Receiving Authority Use | Gross Wt (kg) of goods 15 | Cube (m³) of goods 16

Net Wt (kg) of goods 16A

MUST BE COMPLETED FOR FULL CONTAINER/VEHICLE LOADS:-

† CORRECT TECHNICAL NAME, PROPRIETARY NAMES ALONE ARE NOT SUFFICIENT.

CONTAINER/VEHICLE PACKING CERTIFICATE 17 It is declared that the packing of the container has been carried out in accordance with the provisions shown overleaf

Name of Company

Signature | Date
of person responsible for packing container

DANGEROUS GOODS DECLARATION I hereby declare that the contents of this consignment are fully and accurately described above by the correct technical name(s) (proper shipping name(s)), that the shipment is packaged in such a manner as to withstand the ordinary risks of handling and transport by sea, having regard to the properties of the goods to be carried, and that the goods are classified, packaged, marked and labelled in accordance with the requirements of the Merchant Shipping (Dangerous Goods) Regulations 1981 as currently amended I further declare that if appropriate the goods are classified, packaged and marked to comply with the requirement of the European Agreement concerning the International Carriage of Dangerous Goods by Road (ADR) and of Annex 1 (RID) to the International Convention concerning the Carriage of Goods by Rail (CIM) or special arrangements made between the contracting parties to these Agreements

The shipper must complete and sign box 19.

Total Gross weight of goods | Total Cube of goods

Prefix & Container/Vehicle Number 18 | Seal Number(s) 18A | Container/Vehicle Size & Type 18B | Tare Wt (kg) as marked on CSC plate 18C | Total of boxes 15 and 18C 18D

DOCK/TERMINAL RECEIPT Received the above number of packages/containers/trailers in apparent good order and condition unless stated hereon. RECEIVING AUTHORITY REMARKS | Name of Shipper preparing this note & telephone no. 19

Hauler's Name | NAME/STATUS OF DECLARANT

Vehicle Reg No. | DATE

DRIVER'S SIGNATURE | SIGNATURE & DATE | Signature of Declarant

890 *Mark 'X' as appropriate. If box 5 is not completed the company preparing this note may be held liable for payment of port charges. Non-completion of any boxes is a subject for resolution by the contracting parties. TATE FREIGHT FORMS 0906 567687

Figure 8.1 *A dangerous goods note*

ferry, maritime regulations apply, in particular the Dangerous Substances in Harbour Areas Regulations, effective from June 1987. These rules include the stipulation that the port authority must be notified of every shipment of hazardous goods in advance. Every port has different local regulations but, with the possible exception of explosives, it is feasible to ship most other types of hazardous goods on Ro-Ro ferries as long as all the rules are followed. The shipping companies will often insist that dangerous goods are shipped on freight-only vessels. This is convenient as many Ro-Ro services are freight only and even on the popular routes, such as Dover–Calais, there are a certain number of freight-only sailings every day.

The procedures surrounding the carriage of dangerous goods by road are similar to the air and sea regulations. The ADR regulations have been accepted by all countries in Western Europe, and some in Eastern Europe, and they permit the trucking of dangerous goods across national frontiers. For the shipper, the most important task is to provide a full and accurate description of the goods to the haulier who can then make all the necessary arrangements for the road and sea part of the journey.

Groupage operators will accept dangerous goods but again must be advised well in advance, so that suitable arrangements for temporary storage, handling and shipment can be made. The method of packaging for dangerous goods is regulated by the Road Traffic (Carriage of Dangerous Substances in Packages) Regulations which were implemented in 1987. Known as the PGR regulations, these rules set down the acceptable standards of packaging for hazardous cargo.

Exhibition goods

Exhibitions around the world are becoming increasingly popular as a way of marketing products overseas. As many UK exporters are eligible for a subsidy from the British Overseas Trade Board (now absorbed into the DTI), most British exporters will be involved in an overseas exhibition from time to time.

The perennial nightmare for any exhibitors is the thought of their expensive stand attracting special attention just because it is empty! Such disasters can be avoided by adopting a few basic rules and making sure that certain procedures are followed on every occasion. The first rule is to allow sufficient time for goods to reach the exhibition hall and not to underestimate the time required. If, for example, the exhibition is being held in Hong Kong, and the intention is to send the goods by sea, the transit time is between 25 and 35 days depending on the shipping line used. No line, however, operates a daily service, so goods will be held at the dock for several days. Once the vessel has arrived in Hong Kong, allow a few days for

103

delivery to the exhibition hall and erection of the stand. The same rules apply to air freight. Although much quicker, it is likely that the cargo will wait at the airport for one or two days before departure, particularly if the consignment is large and cannot be accommodated on a passenger flight.

The main additional documentation requirement for exhibition goods is an ATA carnet (see Figure 8.2), often referred to simply as a carnet. The carnet is a widely recognised international document which permits goods to be imported temporarily into a foreign country without the payment of any import duty or taxes. If the goods are then sold, normal taxes become payable. Failure to have a carnet available may lead to delays, and the shipper will certainly have to pay the appropriate duty and taxes, even if this is refunded once the goods have left the country again.

Carnets are issued by chambers of commerce who can also advise exhibitors of any other required documents. The use of a carnet does not preclude the need for the normal forms such as invoices, packing lists and certificates of origin. As with all other shipments, local conditions vary and exhibitors should consult *Croner's Reference Book for Exporters*.

Major exhibition organisers overseas will usually nominate a freight forwarder as the official forwarder for the event, and this company or their UK agent will approach exhibitors direct and offer their services. There is no obligation to use the official forwarder, but you may find this service more convenient. The alternative is to seek out a firm which specialises in handling exhibition shipments. Several highly reputable freight forwarders, such as the Lep Group, have specialised divisions which deal exclusively with exhibitions around the world. Resident experts can advise on all transport and documentation aspects regarding the shipment and provide an all-inclusive price for the despatch and return of the goods. The wide experience of such firms means that their customers avoid the heartbreak of an empty stand.

UK importers will also want to receive exhibition goods occasionally for a UK event. The responsibility for arranging the shipment will often be taken by the overseas supplier, and again it is important to ensure that a carnet accompanies the goods when they come into the UK and upon their departure.

Furniture removals and personal effects

The international nature of business has led to British personnel working overseas as well as many more foreign nationals coming to work in the UK. Even small companies establish a subsidiary company abroad and choose to fill some of the positions with people from the head office.

These employees will want to move their household and personal

RE-EXPORTATION COUNTERFOIL No. _____ 1 _____
SOUCHE DE REEXPORTATION NO.

A.T.A. CARNET No. ▓▓▓▓
CARNET A.T.A. No. **SF/2/648**

1. The goods described in the General List under item No(s).
   Les marchandises énumérées à la liste générale sous le(s) no(s)

   temporarily imported under cover of importation voucher(s) No(s)
   importées temporairement sous le couvert du/des) volet(s) d'entrée no(s).
   of this carnet have been re-exported *) / du présent carnet, ont été réexportées *)

2. Action taken in respect of goods produced but not re-exported *)
   Mesures prises à l'égard des marchandises répresentées mais non réexportées *)

3. Action taken in respect of goods not produced and not intended for later re-exportation *)
   Mesures prises à l'égard des marchandises non représentées et non destinées à une ré-exportation ultérieure *)

4. Registered under reference No. *) / Enregistré sous le no *)

| (Customs office) | (Place / Lieu) | (Date / Date) | (Signature and stamp) |
| (Bureau de douane) | *) Delete if inapplicable / Biffer s'il y a lieu | | (Signature et Timbre) |

RE-EXPORTATION VOUCHER No. ___ 1
VOLET DE REEXPORTATION No.

A.T.A. CARNET No. ▓▓▓▓
CARNET A.T.A. No. **SF/2/648**

A) This carnet is valid until / ce carnet est valable jusqu' au _____ **August 14, 1989** _____ inclusive. / inclus.

Issued by / Délivré par   **FINLAND   Likkisepänkuja 4, 02600 Espoo, Finland**

Holder / Titulaire   **Unda Oy, Ahventie 4 A, 02170 Espoo, Finland**

Represented by *) / Représenté par *) ■■■■■■■■■■■■■■■■■■■■■■■■

B) Re-exportation declaration / Déclaration de réexportation

1. I, / Je soussigné, _____ , *)

   duly authorised by *) / dûment autorisé par *) _____ , *)

   declare that I am re-exporting the goods enumerated in the list overleaf and described in the General List under item.
   déclare réexporter les marchandises énumérées à la liste figurant au verso et reprises à la liste général sous le (s)
   No(s)
   No(s) _____ , which were temporarily imported under cover of importation voucher(s)
   qui ont été importées temporairement sous le couvert du/des) volet(s)
   No(s) _____ of this carnet. *)
   d'entrée no(s) du présent carnet. *)

2. Particulars concerning goods produced but not intended for re-exportation *)
   Indications concernant les marchandises représentées, mais non destinées à la réexportation *)

3. Particulars concerning goods not produced and not intended for later re-exportation *)
   Indications concernant les marchandises non représentées et non destinées à un réexportation ultérieure *)

4. In support of this declaration, I present the following documents *)
   A l'appui de mes déclarations, je présente les documents suivants *)

5. Identifying particulars concerning: / Indications concernant:
   a) packages (number, kind, marks, etc.) *)
      Nombre, nature, marques, etc., des colis *)
   b) means of transport *) / Moyen de transport *)

| (Place / Lieu) | (Date / Date) | (Signature / Signature) |

C) Clearance on re-exportation / Dédouanement à la réexportation

1. The goods referred to in paragraph 1 of the above declaration have been re-exported. *)
   Les marchandises visées au paragraphe 1 de la déclaration ci-dessus ont été réexportées. *)

2. Action taken in respect of goods produced but not re-exported *)
   Mesures prises à l'égard des marchandises représentées, mais non réexportées *)

3. Action taken in respect of goods not produced and not intended for later re-exportation *)
   Mesures prises à l'égard des marchandises non représentées et non destinées à une réexportation ultérieure *)

4. Registered under reference No. *) / Enregistré sous le no. *)

5. This voucher must be forwarded to the Customs office of *)
   Le présent volet devra être transmis au bureau de douane de *)

Figure 8.2 *An ATA carnet*

belongings abroad. Such jobs are best left to professional household removers who will come along to estimate the cost of the job and look after all the packing, documentation and transport. Several quotations should be obtained as removal costs can vary widely. Packing is extremely important and removal firms have the expertise which ordinary transport operators lack. Removals can be organised worldwide; the choice and mode of transport will be governed by cost and speed factors.

Often a shipment of personal effects comprises only a suitcase or a piece of furniture. This can be shipped through an established operator who will send it together with other goods. When obtaining a freight quotation, it is advisable to ascertain exactly whether the service offered is a full door-to-door service or whether the consignment will be left on the quay. A careful list should be made of every item included in a shipment. Pilferage of personal effects is, alas, far too common, and any insurance claim must be supported with a correct and detailed inventory. One copy of the contents of each case should be slipped into the inside of the case, one copy can be given to the forwarder; and another copy should be retained by the shipper.

Gift services

Goodwill gestures grease the flow of international trade and companies like to send gifts to important customers. The height of the gift season is, of course, Christmas, when it is possible to hand the whole job over to a specialised gift distributor who will have their own shipping arrangements. Another easy option is to select a gift which can be sent through the post. For more ambitious items, it is best to select a reputable service to the country in question.

The main disadvantage of sending a gift abroad is the possibility that the recipient may have to pay customs duty and local taxes before receiving it. Whatever the sum involved, this devalues the gesture and can cause embarrassment.

Hanging garments

In recent years, clothes have been transported as hanging garments. This means that clothes are put on to hangers which are themselves hooked to clothes rails. In most cases, the complete rails are moved in and out of lorries and containers, or hanging garments are given a special sealed unit which moves from door to door. Hanging garment transport is particularly appropriate for dresses, skirts, suits, coats and trousers. Other items tend to be folded into cartons before shipment. Many retailers now insist on supplies being delivered as hanging garments. This means that the clothes rail can be moved directly on to the sales floor, and so a great deal of time and space is saved.

Hanging garment services are available for both exporters and importers of clothes. Within Europe special vehicles take UK designs to the Continent and return to the UK with the latest Continental fashions. Clothes are also sent in vast quantities to the USA and imported from the Far East, and there are hanging garment services by sea and air linking the UK with these two parts of the world. Many freight forwarders operate a hanging garment service but their credentials should be checked before use. Clothes are a valuable and delicate commodity and should be handled by experts – no one wants the latest *haute couture* sharing container space with leaking oil cans!

Motor cars

The transport of motor cars overseas can be easy, particularly if the destination is elsewhere in Europe or in the Middle East. The car can be driven across the Channel and then officially imported into the overseas market.

Large quantities of cars are sent abroad by major motor manufacturers and they have their own sophisticated distribution arrangements. Yet there are now smaller firms which are involved in the motor industry on an international scale and they have to move abroad up to 12 vehicles at a time either for resale or perhaps for an auction.

Car transporters are road vehicles which have been designed to carry built-up motor cars; these lorries are undergoing continuous refinement so that they can take larger numbers of cars per journey. They can provide a door-to-door service, although this is expensive as the specialised equipment normally has to return empty.

Rail is another possibility and is likely to become more important after the opening of the Channel Tunnel. Special rail wagons take the cars to the Channel port where the cars are driven on to the ferry. On the other side of the Channel, the cars are loaded on to rail wagons which take them to the station nearest to their destination. For destinations outside Europe, cars can be loaded on to Ro-Ro ferries (see Chapter 5) or taken on most conventional and some containerised services. A single motor car can easily be driven into a container and transported that way.

Motor cars also pour into the UK from overseas. The established foreign vehicle distributors have their well-tried arrangements, but smaller companies can use a similar combination of road, rail and sea. In many countries motor cars are subject to special regulations and taxes and, before allowing them into the country, customs authorities check the vehicles to ensure that they comply with local regulations. In the USA, for example, exhaust emission controls are far tighter than in Europe, and it is essential to ensure that the vehicle meets these standards before it is shipped.

Chapter 9

Terms of Sale

Introduction

The terms of sale appear somewhere in the documentation whenever goods are exported or imported. They may have been agreed between the buyer and seller after a discussion, or either party may have decided on them unilaterally – a less ideal solution.

The terms of sale are frequently included in a quotation for an order and are almost always shown on the invoice. The key words to look out for are ex works, FOB or CIF which are the most commonly used abbreviations. Typically on an invoice, one might see any one of the following terms: FOB UK Port, FOB Dover, FOB Milan, ex works Cambridge, CIF Paris, CIF Sydney. None of these examples should be used, as most of them are either confusing or inaccurate. More misunderstandings and errors are made about terms of sale than about almost any other aspect of international transport. Yet arriving at the correct terms of sale is an important part of marketing strategy and can help to establish goodwill with customers overseas. It is well worth the effort to understand the options available, and then to change one's terms of delivery to bring them up to date with modern transport developments. Terms of delivery should not be confused with terms of payment which are the agreed arrangements for settling the account.

Incoterms

Many years ago, the International Chamber of Commerce (ICC) published some rules for the interpretation of trade terms. These are the Incoterms and they are widely used throughout the world. There is no legal obligation to use them, but it is surprising how many companies do not. Their use does make international trade far easier as all the obligations of the buyer and seller are clearly set out in the *ICC Guide to Incoterms*. While Incoterms simplify international trade, the American interpretation of them is different in several respects from the UK understanding so care should be taken.

The ICC issued a revised Incoterms in spring 1990. This revision, known as Incoterms 1990, includes several changes, the most important being the phasing out of some of the terms of sale.

Apart from the Incoterms described in this section, many companies still apply the customary terms of sale. This can lead to confusion, as terms like 'franco domicile' include different elements of the freight movement and there is no broad agreement on the matter. The great advantage of the Incoterms is that they provide standard interpretations; their setting out has been simplified in 1990 with the aim of gaining wider acceptance.

Incoterms within Europe

The commonest Incoterms used are Free on Board (FOB) and Cost, Insurance and Freight (CIF). These two terms should apply to sea transport only, although they are also widely used for shipment by air and road. Nevertheless, one area which still leads to confusion among UK traders is the use of Incoterms within Europe. Most freight within Europe moves by road on a door-to-door basis, but many companies have not changed their terms of sale to take account of this development. Typically, a shipment destined to Paris will be sold on 'FOB UK Port' terms. In reality, the trailer will load at the consignor's factory or at a groupage depot, and stop for a few moments at the Channel port before continuing on the Ro-Ro ferry. The truck operator offers a door-to-door price for the consignment, including the sea freight, road tolls, fuel and all other charges. Dividing the shipment at the Channel port is artificial as there is no actual break in the journey. It means that in theory the consignee can request that the goods are transferred to another carrier at the port – an impractical suggestion.

Similarly, importers often receive from their European suppliers documents which carry the annotation 'FOB Frontier' or 'Franco Frontier'. Stopping at the frontier between, for example, West Germany and Belgium for a trailer travelling to Zeebrugge is an artificial break and not an appropriate place for responsibility for the goods and charges to pass over to another party.

Ex works

When delivering goods to a domestic customer, there is usually no detailed discussion about the terms of delivery. If the customer is in Newcastle and the goods are being manufactured in Cardiff, it is usually the responsibility of the supplier in Cardiff to ensure that the goods are delivered to Newcastle. The manufacturer has a number of options available (see Chapter 2), but it is most unlikely that the customer will be telephoned and simply told that the goods are at his disposal in a factory hundreds of miles away.

However, this is the philosophy behind ex works terms which are still used widely by many British exporters. If the supplier is situated in Sheffield, the correct terminology for an ex works sale is 'ex works Sheffield'. Under Incoterms this means that the seller is not responsible for loading the goods, although he will, in most circumstances, carry out this task at no charge, acting as the agent for the buyer. Some difficult companies adhere rigidly to the Incoterms interpretation and refuse to become involved in loading the shipment. This only adds a further layer of practical problems.

The effect of an ex works contract is to pass the responsibility for organising the delivery of the goods on to the customer. The customer is often situated literally thousands of miles away and cannot be expected to be familiar with the various transport options available. The outcome is that the consignee frequently nominates a freight forwarder in his own country to handle the shipment and this company has no reliable counterpart in the UK. At best, the shipment can be delayed and, at worst, the goods are handed over to an unreliable company and are received by the customer late and damaged.

In legal terms, this may not matter as under an ex works contract the responsibility passes to the consignee before the shipment is loaded. Yet commercially such a strategy is disastrous and not an intelligent way to obtain repeat business. In addition, shipping difficulties also lead to payment problems. Frequently, ex works shipments are delayed – sometimes for only a few days, but for more distant destinations possibly for a few weeks – as the nominated forwarder may choose the slowest shipping line to save money. Whenever there is a delay in shipment, delay in payment almost inevitably follows. So the exporter is faced not only with commercial embarrassment but also potential financial loss.

Some foreign customers react to ex works shipments by sending routing orders to their UK suppliers. The routing order normally instructs the UK supplier to contact a particular company when the goods are available. Routing orders are widely resented because frequently the forwarder is located in Cardiff with the supplier in Newcastle, and even arranging to collect the goods involves inordinate delay. The overseas customer is unaware of all these problems because of his ignorance of UK geography; the choice of forwarder is based on local considerations. The routing order can also lead to chaos in the despatch bay. One large exporter used to sell goods to over 50 companies around the world on an ex works basis. This meant being in touch with over 40 freight forwarders, each of whom had their own van collecting one small consignment at a time. The office staff also grew tired of repeating the same instructions to so many different people! The inefficiency of the system and the high costs of collecting individual items eventually forced the company to review its entire distribution system.

Manufacturers must try to avoid selling on ex works terms. In some markets, particularly Comecon countries and other countries where foreign exchange is strictly rationed, selling ex works is mandatory and may even be a condition of obtaining an order. Yet for business throughout Western Europe, North America, the Far East and most of the Middle East where the bulk of UK trade is destined, ex works contracts are a sign of weakness and are not recommended for those companies wanting to establish a presence in an overseas market. The ex works contract is a declaration by the exporter that the goods will be manufactured, but whether, when and in what condition they are received overseas is of no interest to the exporter.

Ex works contracts are still too prevalent among UK manufacturers, while such terms are virtually unknown among European competitors who long ago offered their customers delivery to the front door. It is perhaps not surprising that the UK share of world trade has declined consistently as the ex works philosophy still has many adherents throughout British industry.

Free on Board (FOB)

This is still the most popular term of sale for many UK exporters. Precise data are difficult to obtain, but some studies suggest that as much as 60 per cent of UK exports are sold on ex works or FOB terms. FOB should be used only for deep-sea movements, although this does not prevent FOB from being applied to all kinds of different traffic. Using FOB for freight movements within Europe is misleading, as previously explained (page 110).

Under FOB terms, the seller is responsible for packing and delivering the consignment on board a vessel which has been nominated by the buyer. The seller's responsibility for the goods continues until the goods have passed the ship's rail. Under an FOB contract, the port of departure will also usually be nominated, so the expression used is 'FOB Felixstowe' or 'FOB Hull'.

Exporters who ship FOB terms are passing the responsibility for shipment to their customers overseas. The same criticisms levelled against ex works contracts can be applied equally to FOB – delays are not the responsibility of the exporter but will affect the future relationship. This is particularly the case with deep-sea shipments as the consignee may choose a reliable line or a poor one. For example, an exporter selling on FOB terms to Hong Kong cannot nominate the shipping line. There are at any time anything up to 15 lines shipping directly from the UK to Hong Kong, plus many others which ship via other European ports. Transit times can vary between 21 and 45 days. The Hong Kong customer may choose deliberately (or inadvertently) the slowest line, but the effect of this choice will almost certainly delay payment for the goods, and may also jeopardise future business if the consignee is unaware of the full implications of the choice.

FOB can also lead in many cases to higher UK costs for exporters. Taking the example of Hong Kong, most vessels depart from Felixstowe, Tilbury or Southampton. An exporter based in South Wales will almost certainly find it cheaper to send goods to Southampton rather than to one of the east coast ports. This is not a consideration of the consignee who may nominate a Continental port (FOB Antwerp, FOB Hamburg, FOB Rotterdam), in which case the exporter may face even higher costs to send the goods over to the Continent.

Importers who buy goods on FOB terms are in a position to nominate the carrier. For deep-sea traffic, FOB terms do not pose any real problem as the natural break in the journey occurs at the port of shipment. This is quite different from the position regarding traffic from the rest of Europe where FOB terms for importers do not make a great deal of sense.

Free carrier (FRC)

FRC is the Incoterm which should be used in place of FOB when goods are travelling by road. Under an FRC contract, the exporter will arrange to deliver the goods to a depot nominated by the buyer, and it is the buyer who will be responsible for the freight charges. Usually the place for handing over the goods is a freight forwarder's depot, and the forwarder will have an established service to the country of destination. The charges for delivering the goods to the depot are for the exporter's account.

Free carrier terms are only used occasionally, although their lack of use has arisen more from ignorance than any other factor. Companies which despatch goods overseas by trailer still tend to use the beloved but incorrect FOB. FRC terms have the same disadvantage as FOB terms in that the consignee overseas may direct his supplier in Glasgow to deliver the goods to a depot in the south of England. After a few calculations, the exporter will probably discover that it is cheaper to use a locally based service and pay the freight rather than the relatively expensive inland cartage charge.

As part of the Incoterms 1990 revision, FOB Airport (FOA), Free on Rail (FOR) and Free on Truck (FOT) have been dropped, and replaced by FRC. This means that FRC now covers rail, air, road and sea.

Cost and Freight (CFR)

Under a CFR contract, the freight is arranged and paid for by the buyer. A CFR contract should only apply to goods sent by sea, and the terms of delivery will always include a named port of delivery. CFR should not be used for trailer traffic but could be used, for example, for a shipment by sea to Mombasa. This means that the exporter is responsible for the freight to Mombasa as well as the unloading from the vessel on to the quay. The risk for the goods passes to the consignee when the shipment crosses over the ship's rail.

Cost, Insurance and Freight (CIF)

The only difference between a CIF contract and CFR concerns insurance. The seller is responsible for insuring the goods, although only basic cover is normally required to fulfil CIF conditions. CIF terms of sale are much more common than CFR because, if the buyer arranges the freight, he will also want to insure the goods.

CIF is widely used for freight movements by road, although again this is an incorrect use of Incoterms – the correct equivalent is Freight Carriage and Insurance Paid (CIP). CFR and CIF terms are used for deep-sea traffic when the exporter wants to control the routeing.

Freight Carriage Paid (DCP)

DCP terms of sale apply mainly to road transport, and the exporter takes the responsibility for the goods to a pre-arranged point. For a road movement, these terms will appear as, for example, 'DCP Paris'. DCP terms allow the exporter to nominate the carrier and control the principal part of the journey.

The advantage of DCP terms is that the exporter is providing a partial delivery service to the customer. The buyer in Paris does not have to worry about how the goods will reach Paris, and the exporter will, it is hoped, choose an efficient service to satisfy both parties' requirements.

DCP terms should not, however, be confused with Delivery Duty Paid (DDP) terms of sale. In the above example of the shipment to Paris, the buyer will still pay for the delivery charge from the Paris depot to the consignee's warehouse, French customs formality charges, duty and VAT. Even if the consignee is located in the Paris agglomeration, the local costs can be high and may even exceed the costs of sending the goods to Paris. The reason for this is that once a package is treated individually, the costs are far higher than when the consignment is part of a groupage load.

The other requirement for companies selling on DCP terms is to study a map before despatch. This may seem an obvious suggestion, but knowledge of geography is not always used to its best advantage when shipments are being arranged. Continuing with the example just cited, the consignee may be situated in the south of France rather than Paris. Many exporters fail to study a map, and establish a rule that French traffic is sold 'DCP Paris'.

France is a far larger country than the UK, and the distance between Paris and Marseilles, the port on the Mediterranean, is about 775 kilometres (485 miles) so any customer in that area of France would be obliged to pay some very high local delivery costs to bring the goods from Paris.

It would be far simpler for the exporter to introduce some flexibility into the distribution system and sell the goods 'DCP Marseilles', and use a groupage service which goes directly to Marseilles. The freight charges will be higher to take account of the longer distance, but the local costs for the importer will be sharply reduced, so making the product more competitive overall. The transit time will also be reduced.

Freight Carriage and Insurance Paid (CIP)

CIP terms of sale are similar to DCP conditions with the exception that the seller must also make sure that the goods are insured. Unlike CIF terms, under CIP the shipper must ensure that the insurance cover is adequate, and the consignee must be informed about the nature of the cover arranged.

Delivered Duty Paid (DDP)

This is at the opposite end of the spectrum from ex works. Under DDP terms the shipper pays for all charges until the goods arrive at the customer's door. The charges incurred by the exporter include all the preliminary costs, export documentation, freight, import documentation, final delivery and duty and taxes. DDP is universally applicable whatever the method of transport used.

The term 'franco domicile' is frequently heard instead of DDP and, although franco domicile is not a recognised Incoterm, and so incorrect, it is often understood to mean the same as DDP. DDP is expressed as 'DDP Brussels' which means that all the costs are accepted by the shipper. In practice, many exporters want to control the transport from door to door, but do not want to incur the customs formalities charges or pay duty or VAT. In these cases, the term DDP has to state what is excluded and 'DDP excluding customs clearance' or 'DDP excluding duty and taxes' are used.

Exporters may not want to involve themselves in clearance and other charges because the rates for clearance vary from country to country. In some places clearance costs are based on the value of the goods, and taking on responsibility for costs incurred in a distant land is rather like signing a blank cheque! In addition, many importers have a special arrangement with their nominated local freight forwarder and would possibly balk at having their traffic cleared by an agent nominated by another party.

115

The question of duty payment hardly arises for traffic within the EC and EFTA trading blocs, but goods for other countries are liable to import duty. If the exporter chooses to pay the duty, it removes the burden from the importer and may make the product more competitive and attractive. Yet the duty still has to be paid and, if the exporter is paying the duty, will surely add an appropriate amount to his invoice to cover the outlay. The question of paying duty on behalf of one's customers then becomes purely a commercial question and is only worthwhile if the gesture creates a competitive advantage.

VAT is widely used in Europe and it is extremely rare for exporters to offer to pay the VAT on behalf of their customers. Because VAT is passed down the distribution chain, the VAT paid on imports is classified as an output which can be carried forward until the trading period ends. If the UK exporter pays the VAT, the amount of foreign VAT paid is not allowed as far as VAT liability in the UK is concerned. The UK exporter has, therefore, taken on further expenses which the customer overseas could have in any case offset. So in almost every case DDP terms should exclude VAT.

Under DDP terms the exporter takes on full responsibility for ensuring that the consignment reaches the customer. This means that the trader chooses the method of transport and the carrier, and selects the service which meets the requirements of all parties. Marketing-led companies will almost certainly base their distribution system on DDP conditions, even if liabilities such as duty, formalities and VAT are excluded. DDP is the only way to ensure total control of distribution and so provide your customer with a consistent level of service.

There are certainly many UK companies which have switched to DDP terms and seen their flow of orders increase substantially. The argument is that customers overseas are more likely to order goods from suppliers who provide a door-to-door service than from those who are content to leave orders languishing on a quayside in the expectation that the consignee will arrange the transport.

Using DDP terms also provides the customer with better cost control. The exporter can issue an all-inclusive price list whereas, if goods are sold on ex works or other terms, the consignee has to include an unspecified and often uncertain amount for freight. The amount chosen may be inaccurate, and this error will lead to uncompetitive pricing if the amount was too high or to financial embarrassment if the freight allowance was too low.

Wide use of DDP terms also allows the exporter to investigate the freight options available and select the most appropriate one for each customer. Switching to DDP terms does not mean that expenses overall necessarily rise. The amounts spent on freight will increase, but the additional costs will be compensated by more orders and by the establishment of a close relationship with a small number of freight forwarders. Instead of losing control of traffic, the shipper can promise a forwarder a certain volume of business and therefore perhaps obtain a keener freight rate. Instead of a forwarder collecting one consignment, he might collect several every day for different destinations; this immediately reduces collection costs and congestion at the factory. The more traffic given to a forwarder, the more important the account becomes, and so when a crisis shipment arises, which from time to time it inevitably does, the chosen freight forwarder will be happy to assist without exploiting the situation.

The other beneficiary of DDP terms is a company's cash flow. When goods are delivered more efficiently, invoices will be paid earlier and there will be less need to borrow money while awaiting payment. Even the recalcitrant customer can be pressurised earlier and, if delivery is more reliable, the credit control department cannot be fobbed off by excuses about delays in transit.

DDP terms are more appropriate within Europe than for deep-sea traffic where CFR and CIF are the nearest equivalents. DDP conditions will be used more widely with the approach of the Single European Market. Within the UK, domestic sales are normally made on DDP terms and no customer will accept otherwise. Already many Continental exporters supply their UK customers on DDP terms with the UK importers just settling the VAT liability and paying for customs clearance. UK exporters should now begin to imitate their Continental competitors.

Other Incoterms

Shippers will come across other Incoterms which are used less frequently.

Free Alongside Ship (FAS)
This Incoterm falls between ex works and FOB as the consignee has the responsibility of loading the goods on to the vessel. The exporter arranges the delivery to the dockside.

FOB Airport (FOA)
Used only for air freight traffic, the exporter has to ensure that the goods are put at the disposal of the airline or agent at the nominated airport. From that moment, the charges and responsibility pass to the consignee. FOA has been replaced by FRC from the summer of 1990.

Free on Rail/Free on Truck (FOR/FOT)
These terms are only applicable for transport by rail (see Chapter 3) and the responsibility for loading under FOR or FOT remains with the exporter.

FOR and FOT are the rail equivalent of the road FRC. To add to the confusion, many road operators use FOT as they believe that the truck is a road trailer. This is quite incorrect and FOT and FOR only apply to rail movement. FOR and FOT have also been replaced by FRC.

Other terms

There are several other terms which are even more rarely used – ex ship (EXS), ex quay (EXQ) and Delivered at Frontier (DAF). A full explanation can be obtained from the *ICC Guide to Incoterms*.

Conclusion

Terms of sale are a neglected part of a marketing strategy. In many companies, bold plans fail because something goes wrong 'with the transport' and goods do not reach their destination according to plan. This kind of disaster affects future prospects, and often the original problem arises because the terms of sale have not been integrated into the overall marketing plan. Sales representatives rarely talk about the terms of sale when they are with a customer and so ignore an opportunity to foster a better working relationship. Terms of sale are important and should be used as a competitive weapon by small firms.

Chapter 10
Packing and Insurance

Introduction

Packing and insurance are two neglected facets of distribution. There are plenty of experts around who are knowledgeable about these areas, but their expertise has to be linked to those involved with physical distribution. Everyone recognises that goods need packing, but the choice of packing depends on several factors, many unrelated to the goods being packed. Insurance is essential, but most shippers will only start to worry about the small print of the policy when something has gone wrong. Mistakes are avoidable with careful planning.

The purpose of packing

Packing is intended to protect goods during transit from all types of different hazards. Apart from the additional work which results from poor packing, a sales strategy looks unconvincing when customers receive damaged goods. Cargo in transit is threatened by natural phenomena, mainly the weather, and by man-made problems which include pilferage. Other threats include damage to a consignment because of its proximity to another shipment.

Packing is an integral part of the distribution chain, so the packaging should be designed to maximise the use of the container, trailer or air freight container. In this area there are great opportunities for shippers to save considerable amounts of money. Many trailers and containers depart with a full load but in fact the customer is paying for the transport of air. If the inside of a trailer is 2.2 metres in height and a shipper is loading cartons, each one of which is 1.2 metres in height, only one layer of cartons can be loaded on to the unit. The trailer will depart with a full 1 metre of space along the complete length of the trailer. In terms of the loading capacity of a standard 12 metre tilt trailer, this empty space represents about 40 per cent of the total available capacity. This is a simple example, and there are other factors which may preclude the optimisation of the trailer, including the weight limits and the actual type of goods being shipped. Yet many exporters and importers do not attempt to consider their packing requirements in the light of their pattern of distribution, and in many cases a consideration of this problem and a redesign of their packaging would save a great deal of money. Before quoting for every new contract, traders should consider how the packing and transport aspects are linked.

Influences on packing

The influences on packing are many and varied. The value of the goods is an important consideration and normally the higher the value, the better the packing.

Type of transport

The type of transport must be considered. The modern container has allowed packing for sea transport to become less rigorous as the goods are no longer handled during transit. On the other hand, packing for container transport has to take account of the changes in temperature encountered *en route*. Goods leaving the UK for Australia in winter may first be subject to cold or freezing temperatures; later, as the vessel crosses the Equator, the sun beats down on the containers, heating the contents of the units.

Another influence on packing requirements is the type of handling the goods will receive during their journey.

Although packing for full container load traffic has become less rigorous, smaller consignments, which are being shipped on a consolidation service, will be loaded into the container and unloaded by depot staff. The goods will share space with other types of cargo and the packing must provide sufficient protection. As a general rule, staff at consolidation depots never take as much care of goods as one's own staff who are in any case more aware of how the particular products should be handled. Loading staff at many of these places lack delicacy in their approach to handling freight.

Goods which travel by trailer also require packing and, as with containers, a full load will need less packing than a groupage shipment. The extremes of weather are not such a problem for trailer movements, except for traffic to Scandinavia in winter and to the Middle East, particularly in the hot season. However, the English Channel and the North Sea can become ferocious and severe gales are not uncommon. Trailers are fastened to the sides and deck of Ro-Ro ferries with chains but this does not prevent a load from shifting in the trailer during a storm. Trailers also spend time at Channel ports where a combination of wind, salt water and rain can also damage cargo. Rain is more of a threat to goods on a flat trailer than on a tilt as, although the goods will be covered with a tarpaulin, it is easy for water to seep through and reach the goods. Of course, the use of a flat trailer usually means that the cargo is robust – otherwise a tilt trailer should be used.

120

Type of cargo

The type of cargo is another important consideration in determining the kind of packing required. Smaller shipments generally require superior packing to large shipments since there is a much greater chance of the goods travelling together with other cargo. Aluminium ingots require little packing whereas delicate medical or electronic goods will need excellent protection. Generally, the more fragile the goods, the greater the degree of protection required. Goods travelling air freight usually need less packing than for other modes of transport, and this is an argument for sending the more valuable and delicate shipments by air. The higher freight charge is offset by savings in the packing.

Legal restrictions

There are sometimes legal restrictions on the type of packing allowed to enter a country. For example, in some parts of the world the import of straw is prohibited because of the danger of lodging insects which might then escape. There are also strict rules relating to the packing of dangerous cargo which also has to be marked as agreed by international convention.

Handling of cargo

Before deciding on the type of packing, shippers should check that there are adequate handling facilities throughout the journey. This is especially important for larger pieces of equipment which may require a crane. Some parts of the world do not have sophisticated handling equipment and so larger shipments have to be subdivided into smaller lots.

Although containers are now sent all over the world, many developing countries do not have the skeletal trailers which deliver the containers intact from port to the final destination. Every consignment is, therefore, unloaded and then delivered by other means. The shipper will pack for container movement, unaware that for the last part of the journey much more rigorous packing is required. The solution is to check how the goods will be transported throughout their journey and design the packing for the most vulnerable stage.

Insurance

Certain categories of goods, in particular those subject to pilferage, will have special packing conditions linked to the policy. Failure to follow these conditions may invalidate the policy.

Marketing aspects

The type of packing chosen must also fit in with the marketing strategy. Thus, if the goods are being delivered to shops abroad, it is no use packing the goods in such a way that they cannot be unpacked in a restricted space by one or two people. Outer packing cases and cartons can be designed to make the contents look attractive by carrying the company logo.

Type of packing

Goods can be packed in several different ways.

Unpacked

Some types of cargo are sturdy enough not to require packing in crates or cases. This applies to motor cars, some machinery and bulk commodities such as steel bars. Even though packing is not required, the goods still need protection against sudden movement, vibration, condensation and rain, and it is always advisable to consult a packing company. They will advise on the best method of protection – perhaps securing the machine to a pallet and covering it in shrink wrapping, wrapping the exposed edges of the equipment or coating the item with a protective chemical. These protective measures cost a great deal less than conventional packing which encloses the whole consignment in a wooden crate or case.

Pallet

One of the simplest and most useful inventions is the pallet. Normally made of wood, the pallet is a movable platform and goods are placed on the pallet and then fastened to it. The fastening can be with a metal band for goods in cartons; certain products might be nailed to the pallet. A lot of goods are covered with shrink wrapping which also helps to secure them to the pallet.

The advantage of pallets is that they are relatively cheap and highly manoeuvrable. Forklift trucks load and unload pallets, as every pallet has slots where the forks of the truck enter and lift the entire pallet off the ground. Pallets are reusable and there are companies which hire out pallets on a long-term basis. It is rare for pallets to return to their place of despatch unless special arrangements have been made with the consignee. The tendency is for manufacturers to retain all incoming pallets and use them for exports.

Pallets come in different sizes but the most commonly used are the Euro pallet – 1000 mm × 800 mm, and the UK pallet, slightly larger – 1000 mm × 1200 mm. Because of its popularity, trailer and container manufacturers have tried to design their units to maximise the number of pallets which can be loaded in one unit. The precise load factor will also depend on the height of the goods but, by using a Euro or a UK pallet, shippers are more likely to have a better storage factor than if they use another size. It would be a modest step towards the ideal of 1992 for pallet sizes to be standardised. This has not yet happened, but the standard is likely to be the Euro pallet rather than the UK pallet, if only because the Euro pallet is far more widely used throughout Europe.

Not more than about 1000–1500 kilos of goods should be loaded on one pallet, and even this is too much for certain areas of the world where forklift trucks are unavailable. Forklift trucks themselves have their own capacity limitations and most pallets, shipping on a consolidation service, weigh less than 1000 kilos. The height limitation depends on the weight of the cargo and on whether the pallets are going to be stacked on top of one another in the trailer or container.

Bags

Bags are made from jute, paper and increasingly from synthetic material. They are used for low-value products including harmless chemicals, fertilisers, minerals and animal products. Frequently bags are heaped on to a pallet.

Bags are cheap and disposable, but they provide only minimal protection against water which penetrates through the smallest hole. The contents also sweat in transit. Bags split easily, spilling their contents which are then lost, and there is virtually no protection against pilferage.

Boxes, crates, cases and tea chests

These are the traditional items, made of wood and sometimes metal, used for packing. Shippers who use them will often have the boxes made to order so that their shipments fit tightly inside. Boxes and cases are used mainly for road and sea transport, for both container and conventional shipment, and to a lesser extent in air freight. They offer excellent protection for delicate machinery but the material costs of boxes and cases are high. This method of packing should be used only when absolutely necessary and should not be used as standard packing.

To the cost of the material must be added the time taken to pack the goods. Packing to this high standard should be left to one of the many experienced packing companies. Making and then packing a box or case is both time-consuming and expensive. The work can be completed on site or at a packer's premises.

This type of packing protects the goods well and, if the cargo is delicate and will be travelling over rough roads, a good wooden case is a worthwhile investment. It is also far less liable to pilferage than a carton as the goods are more difficult to reach. The wood is thick and the case is nailed making access difficult. Tea chests are used for household removals and the transport of personal effects. They are inexpensive and inflexible and have stood the test of time.

Cartons

The carton is a popular form of packing, particularly for consumer goods and non-perishable foodstuffs. Cartons are made of cardboard or fibreboard and, as an added protection, the goods inside the carton can be separated by polystyrene particles. Cartons can also be loaded easily on to a pallet. The advantage of using a carton is its price; it is a cheap form of packing, used extensively for road trailer, air and container shipment.

The disadvantage of a carton is its vulnerability to crushing which occurs frequently with groupage shipments surrounded by much heavier items. Cartons are also relatively easy to break into so theft can be a problem. As many cartons are quite small, it is not uncommon for several to disappear while in transit. Customers often have a preference for cartons because the goods are easily available and the carton can be used as part of the point-of-sale activity.

Cartons are, however, unsuitable for conventional shipment for which they do not offer sufficient protection.

Drums and barrels

Drums and barrels are used for the transport of liquids. Drums can be made of metal or plastic and they come in various standard gallon and litre sizes. Chemicals, both hazardous and non-hazardous, are shipped in drums, but great care must be taken to ensure that the product does not corrode the packing. The advantage of a plastic drum is that it is less vulnerable to rust.

Drums and barrels have to be sealed tightly, and there is a risk of leakage and evaporation if the goods are going to a hot climate and of freezing if the destination is a cold one. Drums are also cumbersome to handle on their own. Many shippers load drums on to pallets so they can be moved by a forklift truck.

Shrink wrapping

Shrink wrapping is a widely used technique for the protection of goods. The cartons are stacked on to a pallet and covered with a thick plastic material which is affixed to the goods by the use of a hot air blower. Shrink wrapping offers adequate protection for air freight traffic and, depending on the nature of the goods, for road trailer and container despatch.

Marking of goods

The marking of goods is important – an unmarked consignment will inevitably be mislaid at some stage. Even worse, once unmarked, the goods become virtually untraceable as one carton looks very much like another. At the same time, marking should not reveal any information about the contents of the goods to avoid the risk of theft.

The information on the packing should include the initials of the consignee, the destination town and the number of the carton. So if you were intending to send 10 cartons to Paris, the marking on the third carton would be as follows:

```
SD
PARIS
3 of 10
```

Some companies also include the order number as an additional line but the above example is quite adequate for goods which are going straight to the customer. For the same consignment travelling to a smaller French town, an additional line should be included:

```
SD
TOURS
VIA PARIS
3 of 10
```

The additional line 'via Paris' is inserted to minimise the danger of misdirecting the cargo and, even if the goods are misrouted, the marking will ensure that they are returned to Paris for on-forwarding again to Tours.

In addition to the marking, which should be clearly visible, every package must have the full address of the sender. There are also various agreed international markings (see Figure 10.1) to be used when packages are fragile or when they have to be stacked in a certain way.

The cost of packing

After considering all these factors, companies must decide which type of packing is appropriate for their goods. As well as bearing in mind the actual packing costs, consideration must be given to the wider marketing implications. Packing is an integral part of the production and selling chain and decisions cannot be taken in isolation.

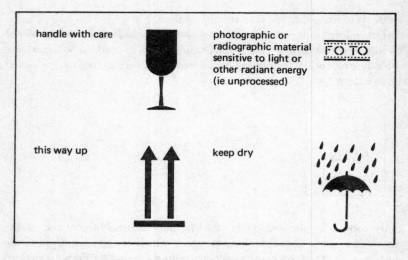

Figure 10.1 *International markings for handling packages*

The reason for insurance

Insuring goods in transit is rarely considered an important priority when arranging shipments. In many cases the question of insurance is not mentioned by either party to the transaction, with both the exporter and the importer believing that the other is arranging cover. Alternatively, there is a naïve belief that adequate cover is provided by the carrier.

Neglecting to insure goods in transit is all very well until something goes wrong. Disaster may strike on the first shipment or the hundredth but at some time an unforeseen event will affect the precious consignment. In transport the main area of risk is damage to goods which can arise from any of a number of reasons; for example vibration, an accident, poor handling or wet. In addition, there is, unfortunately, the ever-present threat of pilferage which may be limited to a small part of the consignment, but it is not unknown for the total contents of trailers or containers to disappear without trace. In certain parts of the world, drivers take it upon themselves to sell the contents of the lorry which they are driving.

Many small companies do not consider insurance until after an incident and it is certainly too late by then. The only outcome will be that future shipments will be insured but, in the meantime, there is a financial loss. The reason for insuring goods is no different from the reason for insuring against any other risk – the shipper is protected against financial loss which may arise through no fault of either the buyer or the seller.

With a few exceptions, transport firms do not insure the goods they convey unless they receive specific instructions from their customers. These instructions should be in writing, so there are no grounds for subsequent confusion if the instructions are not followed and a claim arises.

Type of cover

Insurance can be arranged through a freight forwarder or via an insurance broker. Occasional exporters can instruct their forwarder to insure a specific shipment and the policy will cover a particular journey for one consignment. This policy is often referred to as a single voyage policy and the freight forwarder will debit the premium to the exporter along with the other charges.

Regular exporters are better advised to arrange insurance through a registered insurance broker. The knowledgeable broker will obtain competitive quotations from different sources and advise the client accordingly. The trader will normally be provided with an open cover policy which will provide insurance cover on an annual basis. The quotation will be based on the type of goods, the destinations served and the method of transport. Once an initial deposit has been made, the exporter will complete an insurance certificate in respect of every shipment and forward one of the copies to the broker. The final premium will be assessed at the end of the year when full details of every shipment and the claims record are known. The advantage of open cover is that the shipper has flexibility and will only have to consult the insurance broker for special shipments – when, for instance, goods are being sent to a war zone or when the value of the consignment is higher than normal.

A more restricted version of open cover is the annual premium. Under this policy the consignment has to be declared to the insurance broker prior to shipment. Such an arrangement may apply if most traffic goes to remote parts of the world, but this method of operation is more time-consuming and bureaucratic.

Excess

In common with most types of insurance, transit insurance policies will often offer the option of an excess. In exchange for a lower premium, claims up to a predetermined amount will not be met. The advantage of such an arrangement for the insured is a lower premium and no requirement to process small claims which are in any case administratively expensive to handle. The disadvantage is that a succession of uncovered small claims can be expensive. Every trader must decide whether to accept the excess on offer.

Insurance and terms of delivery

Failure to insure goods often arises because the exporter and the importer both believe that the other party is responsible for arranging the cover. The responsibility for insuring the goods rests with their owner and ownership of the consignment is governed by the terms of sale (see Chapter 9). Thus, under an FOB contract, the exporter is the owner of the goods until they pass over the ship's rails, so it is important to ensure that goods are insured up to this point in the journey. An alternative method of organising matters is for the exporter to arrange for door-to-door insurance and debit the customer a proportion of the premium to cover the journey from the ship's rail through to the final destination. In a CIF contract it is the exporter who is responsible for payment of the freight and for insuring the goods until they reach their destination.

The most important point is that the exporter and importer must liaise to ensure that goods are insured throughout their journey.

Calculation of an insurance premium

Normally goods are insured for the CIF value of the consignment plus 10 per cent of that figure. Using the CIF value means that, in addition to the value of the goods, the freight charges and insurance premium are also covered. The 10 per cent means that, in the event of a total loss, the insured receives some compensation for the expense of processing the claim and for any consequential commercial loss.

For a consignment with a value of £1000, assuming a freight charge of £100 and an insurance rate of 0.75 per cent, the insurance premium is calculated as follows:

Value of goods	£1,000
Freight	100
C & F value	£1,100

To calculate the insurance premium, it is common practice to add a further 10 per cent to the C & F value.

$$£1100 \times \frac{10}{100} = £110$$

This amount is added to the original £1100 so the goods will be insured for £1210. This is the CIF value. Frequently, the CIF value is rounded up to the nearest £10 for low-value shipments and to the nearest £100 or £1000 for larger shipments.

In this case, the premium will be based on an amount of £1210, so the premium will be:

0.75% of £1210 = £9.08

Thus, the premium payable is £9.08 to which may be added a small administration charge which will not amount to more than a few pounds.

There are other ways of calculating insurance premiums, but they involve more complicated formulas and this method, if not totally acceptable to the experts, is widely used.

It is worth noting that the insurance premium of 0.75 per cent is widely quoted to many countries round the world so this example is quite realistic. Many shippers do not realise that transit insurance is available at relatively low cost and the small premiums payable are a low price for peace of mind.

Handling of claims

In the event of a claim, the insured company must notify its insurance agent or freight forwarder immediately. Many insurance policies have a time limitation and any claim not notified within a certain period after the goods have been delivered will be disallowed. At the same time as advising the insurance broker, written notice of an impending claim should be sent to any carrier or freight forwarder involved in handling the consignment. Notification of a claim should always be in writing to avoid any confusion at a later stage.

In many cases the damage incurred will be of a minor nature or indeed non-existent. This can happen when the outsides of cartons are damaged but the contents are still in good condition. Alternatively, in a large consignment of china or glassware, it may be that one or two items are damaged and these are covered by the excess. In every case the insurance broker should be notified, even if full details of the claim are not known at the time. When it is discovered that the damage is non-existent or minimal, the claim can be withdrawn. If this precaution has not been taken, any eventual claim may be disallowed by the passage of time.

The insurance company will usually appoint a surveyor or loss adjuster who will recommend a settlement which is acceptable to both the claimant and the insurer. Loss adjusters are only used for large claims; small claims will often be settled by correspondence, although the insurer has the right to examine the goods in question while the claim is being processed.

It is not often realised that everyone has an interest in minimising the number of claims as they are an important influence on the level of premiums. Insuring goods should not be used as an excuse for negligence in packing or security. The insured company must continue to behave as if the goods were uninsured at all times.

Carrier's liability

When goods are carried by road, sea or air, the carrier has certain liabilities in respect of the goods carried. These responsibilities form part of the international transport conventions and a short study of the conditions will show why independent insurance is required. Exporters cannot rely on the liability or compensation payments of these conventions. The value of goods moving around the world has risen through inflation and other factors. The maximum financial liabilities for loss or damage accepted by the providers of transport have, in many cases, not changed for many years. All this information appears in the conditions of carriage – the small print which no one reads but which can be found on the reverse of most transport documents (see Figure 6.7, page 75).

The CMR Convention

The CMR Convention covers international transport by road, so vehicles travelling between the UK and other parts of Europe operate under CMR conditions. As every trailer has, at some point, to travel by ferry, it is arguable whether the CMR conditions continue to apply when the trailer is at sea. Some experts feel that, in the event of a loss at sea, liability may be in accordance with maritime law rather than the CMR Convention. Containers which travel by road are treated under CMR conditions until they are lifted off at a port or railway station when other conditions will apply.

Under CMR conditions, the limit of compensation is 8.33 Special Drawing Rights (SDR) per kilo of gross weight of the goods lost or damaged. The precise conversion of the SDR will vary daily, and the exchange rate is quoted in the *Financial Times*. Transport charges, duties and other costs are refundable on a pro rata basis.

The Hague Visby Rules

These are the rules governing sea transport which became effective in the UK in 1977. Under these rules, the shipping company must take care to ensure the safe carriage of goods, and in theory the shipping line is liable if goods leave in good condition but arrive damaged.

In practice, however, the shipping lines are protected by a battery of exemptions which make it hard for any claimant to squeeze compensation from them. The exemptions are too long to examine in full but one example indicates the kind of problem facing a potential claimant. Damage by fire, even if the fire was caused by the shipping line's employees, is sufficient defence against a claim.

It is thus difficult to obtain compensation under the Hague Visby Rules. The present limit is either 666.67 SDRs per package or 2 SDRs per kilo. There is no compensation for delay.

The application of the Hague Visby Rules is not universal. Many large trading countries, including the USA and Japan, have not acknowledged these rules, so goods coming from them will be subject to different conditions. Many countries still use the Hague Rules which preceded the Hague Visby Rules. In general terms, the Hague Rules are even more restrictive than the Hague Visby ones.

The Warsaw Convention

The Warsaw Convention was established in 1929 but amended in 1955 and again in 1961. The Convention applies to goods during the time they are in the air between two countries which are signatories to the Convention. The conditions of carriage appear on the back of every air waybill. Compensation is payable at the rate of '250 gold francs of 65.5 milligrams of gold of millesimal fineness 900 per kilo'. As it is difficult to understand this mumbo jumbo, the UK government issues a sterling equivalent from time to time. At the moment, the equivalent is £13.63 per kilo and this includes transport costs and any duty. As with the Hague Visby and CMR limits, this maximum amount does not reflect in any way the value of most consignments.

Freight forwarders' trading conditions

Shippers who use a registered member of the British International Freight Association (BIFA) (Chapter 11) know that the forwarder concerned has met the strict criteria laid down by that body. Registration is granted by the BIFA by providing the company concerned with a registration number which will appear on all stationery and other documents. The 1989 Institute of Freight Forwarders (IFF) trading conditions also appear on the reverse of quotations, certificates of shipments, invoices and other documents.

Using an accredited freight forwarder, however, does not in itself provide the trader with a sufficient level of insurance cover, and goods should be independently insured or cover arranged through the freight forwarder. The same is true for goods which are shipped under a FIATA bill of lading (see Chapter 6) – independent specific insurance is indispensable.

This short summary should explain why the shipper must arrange his own insurance. It is no use relying on the carrier.

Chapter 11

The Role of Freight Forwarders

Introduction

The traditional role of the freight forwarder was simply to act as an agent on behalf of exporters and importers. The forwarder prepared shipping documents for the traffic which was despatched by sea to countries which were then part of the British Empire. The role of freight forwarders began to change as UK trade with the Continent increased, and forwarders now undertake a wide range of different responsibilities, sometimes acting as agents and sometimes as principals.

Shipper's agent

This is the traditional role of the freight forwarder. The trader issues instructions to arrange for the shipment of a consignment to, for example, the USA, and the shipping line and vessel are nominated by the trader. The forwarder liaises with both the shipping line and its customer and may even pay the FOB charges on behalf of the exporter. The bill of lading, however, is made out in the shipper's name.

Forwarder as an adviser to a trader

Many exporters and importers are not interested in the minutiae of international transport and so look to their freight forwarder for advice. This is a role which every forwarder is pleased to fulfil; he is far more likely to be up to date with changes in freight rates, surcharges and shipping or airline schedules. He will also be aware of new options which become available to any particular market as well as any special conditions which restrict access to a destination.

Acting on the instructions of the customer, the forwarder will make a few enquiries and then recommend a particular shipping line or routeing. The forwarder will assist with all the documentation requirements and book the freight with the shipping line, but once again the bill of lading will be made out in the shipper's name. Here too, the freight forwarder is acting as an agent on behalf of the forwarder.

Multi-modal operator

Freight forwarders now operate their own services, and so the forwarder becomes the principal rather than the agent. This is particularly the case for road freight to other parts of Europe. Large freight forwarders, such as Davies Turner or Rockwood International, run their own services to many parts of Europe. Instead of just arranging or recommending a routeing, the forwarder actually becomes involved in the physical movement of the goods.

In this situation the freight forwarder may be the carrier for the whole journey or for only part of the journey, as frequently freight forwarders, even though they market a service under their own name, sub-contract part of the movement to a third party. For the exporter, this blurring of roles does not matter; the freight forwarder is taking responsibility for getting the goods from A to B and any queries or claims must be lodged with him. Large forwarders tend to own some of their equipment. They may own small cartage vehicles or large 12 metre trailers. When a company owns a number of vehicles, it can be classified as an international haulier, and several large companies in the international transport industry regard themselves as international hauliers as well as freight forwarders. The division between an international haulier and a freight forwarder is to a certain extent artificial within Europe. Both parties perform a similar function which is to take responsibility for moving goods from one country to another. Their trading conditions may differ, and this has implications in case of a mishap, such as loss or damage to a consignment.

When a freight forwarder markets an NVOCC service (see Chapter 5) or an air freight consolidation service (see Chapter 4), he is acting as a multi-modal operator. The forwarder will decide on the shipping line or airline to be used, take responsibility for the cargo, and therefore act as the principal.

The easiest way of establishing whether the freight forwarder is acting as an agent or as a principal in any transaction is by looking at the documentation which relates to the movement of the cargo. If the exporter's name appears on an ocean bill of lading or an airline waybill, the forwarder is acting as an agent. If, however, the freight forwarder issues an FIATA bill of lading or a house airway bill, the forwarder is acting as a principal.

The final area of potential confusion is the practice among the freight forwarding industry of smaller forwarders passing traffic on to larger companies who then move the goods themselves. This practice is not even restricted to smaller forwarders; large companies also pass freight on to other firms when they do not have an economic payload or the destination is

133

remote. The passing on of freight applies to full load and groupage traffic, as smaller forwarders will not have sufficient traffic to operate their own services, and will almost certainly not own their own trailers for intra-European business.

This wide adoption of sub-contracting is a useful method of handling freight more efficiently. Instead of every freight forwarder operating a service to New York, smaller companies support the services of larger firms or specialised carriers. The drawback with sub-contracting comes when an exporter learns that his consignment has been passed from one forwarder to another, as each forwarder has to a certain extent misled his predecessor in the chain by accepting the goods even though he did not have a service. As there is nothing intrinsically wrong with sub-contracting, many freight forwarders will freely admit that this is what they do with much of their traffic. Smaller forwarders in particular sub-contract, but other factors in their favour are often more important than this potential disadvantage. One can only ask that forwarders are honest with their customers, and this should be the acid test for exporters and importers. Ask your freight forwarder if his service to, for example, Paris is his own service. As long as the answer is the truth, the fact that the goods may be passed on to another company should not really matter.

Other services

Freight forwarders provide a range of other services which is summarised here.

Customs clearance and documentation

Freight forwarders will organise the customs clearance of goods. This service applies particularly to imports where the procedures are more complicated. At every port and airport in the UK, there are freight forwarders whose main business is to complete customs formalities on behalf of importers. At London's Heathrow Airport, for example, there are hundreds of freight forwarders – for many of them their only business is completing import entries. A freight forwarder who is only involved with customs entries is often referred to as a clearing agent. The charge for completing import formalities will normally be between £30 and £60 depending on the complexity of the entry.

Similarly, at the major Ro-Ro ports, such as Dover or Felixstowe, there are freight forwarders who will look after all the documentation requirements for exports and imports. They will prepare SADs and liaise with HM Customs on behalf of exporters and importers.

Another area of involvement for freight forwarders is the handling of certificates of origin (see Chapter 6). They frequently have to be verified by the embassy of the country concerned in London or stamped by a chamber of commerce. A freight forwarder, in the normal course of business, will be handling several certificates on a daily basis, and so it is easier and far less time-consuming to let the forwarder look after these important but pernickety aspects of international trade.

In all these areas, the freight forwarder has no involvement and therefore no responsibility for the physical movement of the cargo. If goods are lost or damaged, it has nothing to do with the forwarder.

Packing

Many freight forwarders offer to pack goods for export on behalf of their customers (see Chapter 10). The freight forwarder may belong to a group of companies which includes a packing subsidiary or the forwarder may have developed a close working relationship with a local packer. Increasingly, packing is an activity which exporters are happy to pass on to an outside supplier, as it requires specialised skill and also occupies valuable space in a production area.

Some exporters hand over the complete packing and freight forwarding operation to one company, while other firms split the work between independent contractors. In the latter case, the exporter packer is not involved in international transport and cannot be expected to bear responsibility for any problems that may arise.

Warehousing

Warehousing is another activity which exporters and importers require, but more and more of them now prefer to contract it out to third parties. Many freight forwarders operate warehouses which are divided up between goods in transit and goods under long-term storage. As land and premises in most parts of the UK are expensive, manufacturers prefer to devote as large a proportion of their sites as possible to production and, once goods are finished, they store them elsewhere. Freight forwarders receive goods regularly and store them until a complete consignment is available for shipment. Depending on the type of goods, this storage may last anything from a few days to a few weeks.

Goods to be exported are kept in an unbonded warehouse. An unbonded warehouse is one not under customs control. As far as exports are concerned, they do not require a warehouse under customs control unless the goods in question are liable to excise duty – chiefly tobacco and spirits. When goods require storage under customs control, they are kept under bond. Storing goods under bond is of greater interest to importers as, while goods are under bond, importers do not have to pay import duty or VAT. Import duty, particularly if the goods come from other parts of the EC, is almost irrelevant, but postponing the payment of VAT at 15 per cent can be of great assistance to cash flow. VAT is payable when goods are declared to UK customs and, if goods are kept under bond until they are required, payment of VAT is postponed. The regulations concerning bonded storage are in fact more complicated than this brief explanation and further details should be obtained from HM Customs or a freight forwarder.

Many freight forwarders offer a warehousing service to both exporters and importers. The maintenance of a stock control system on behalf of a customer and the distribution of goods may also be included in this service. Again, storage may be part of a total service which includes the physical movement of goods overseas or into the UK from abroad.

With the growing integration of the UK economy with that of other members of the EC, many exporters are now looking at the possibility of storing goods on the Continent. This trend, highlighted by the changes forecast for 1992 (see Chapter 13), means that freight forwarders transport goods from the UK to the Continent and hold them in store until the exporter issues instructions for delivery. Goods can also be kept under bond on the Continent, thus enabling the foreign importer to postpone payment of VAT until the goods are actually required. Having products stored on the Continent allows UK exporters to compete on equal terms with domestic suppliers. Foreign importers appreciate the reassurance of having their essential supplies available on their doorstep.

The storage of goods overseas is an area where it is increasingly common for freight forwarders to provide a service. The actual storage abroad will, in many cases, be sub-contracted but the whole operation can be arranged and handled by a UK forwarder. Alternatively, the enterprising exporter can find a Continental forwarder with storage and distribution facilities and instruct the UK forwarder to deliver the goods to the nominated forwarder abroad.

Insurance

Every freight forwarder will be pleased to insure goods on behalf of customers (see Chapter 10). As an additional service, the premium income generates a little more profit for the forwarder who can often obtain a keener rate based on the total volume of goods shipped.

Exporters and importers should only insure goods with the freight forwarder who is also responsible for the transport of the goods. It is administratively inconvenient to insure freight with one forwarder and ship with another. This disadvantage becomes more apparent in the event of a claim.

Why use a freight forwarder?

There is no obligation for shippers to use freight forwarders to handle their international traffic. It is quite feasible to approach a shipping line directly, obtain a quotation and book the freight. For an air freight shipment, the procedure is not quite so simple, and it is possible that the airline will ask you to book the freight through a forwarder, particularly if the consignment is small and suitable for a consolidation service. Some large companies prefer to negotiate directly with the actual carriers but, for the majority of traders, it is far easier to use a freight forwarder.

The advantage of a freight forwarder is the flexibility and expertise which he has at his disposal. Booking a shipment to Singapore directly with a shipping line will ensure that the consignment moves on its particular service. When the same shipment is handed over to a forwarder, he will ask details about the urgency of the shipment, the acceptable price, and then recommend one or two different shipping lines. Freight forwarders are in contact with all the shipping lines and the interests of their customers will be of paramount importance.

Freight forwarders can advise customers dispassionately because the forwarders make their profits in three ways. Many airlines and shipping lines give freight forwarders a commission for every piece of freight booked. For air freight, this is one of the great benefits of the forwarder having the International Air Transport Association (IATA) licence. For sea freight, forwarders will receive Freight Agent's Commission (FAC) from non-conference shipping lines (see Chapter 5) and this commission is usually between $2\frac{1}{2}$ and $7\frac{1}{2}$ per cent. When freight is booked with conference carriers (see Chapter 5), FAC is normally not available, so the forwarder will add an amount on to the freight or negotiate an 'under the table' rebate with the shipping line.

The second way in which freight forwarders earn a profit is through volume discounts. By adding together the freight which they receive from all their customers to a particular destination, the forwarder can purchase the shipping space or the air freight at a keener rate. This bulk purchasing discount will be partially retained by the forwarder.

The other main source of profit for freight forwarders is from the wide range of ancillary services previously described (see pages 134–136).

Freight forwarders can also remove the headaches of documentation. They can complete many of the forms on behalf of exporters and importers and also help with the forms which have to be completed by the actual trader. Forwarders can provide a door-to-door service so that once the shipper has advised the freight agent that a consignment is available, the forwarder will organise all aspects of the movement, even if this involves the use of sub-contractors. Using a forwarder in this way saves time and money. The forwarder can proceed with one telephone call; if the trader decides to organise the transport, he must spend time arranging every component of the journey.

A freight forwarder can be used purely as a booking agent or to replace a shipping department. Small firms are unlikely to have the full panoply of a shipping office – transport is rather one of many responsibilities held by a senior employee. Some traders have now handed over the complete administration of their international traffic to a freight forwarder. The marketing and selling of the goods still remain the responsibility of the exporter, but the forwarder looks after all aspects of shipping the freight overseas including perhaps the creation of sales invoices and in some cases credit control. The advantage for a shipper is that administrative costs can be saved, particularly if export traffic fluctuates widely during the year. This king of arrangement is not as rare as it once was and the option needs to be studied carefully before commitment. It is more appropriate for smaller companies than for larger ones but can apply equally to importers and exporters.

Choosing a freight forwarder

Like any other sector of industry, freight forwarders come in different sizes – large, medium and small. The quality of their services is also variable. Many provide an excellent service, while there are some whose professionalism leaves room for improvement. Many freight forwarders are now applying for registration under British Standard 5750 (see page 164).

The structure of the UK forwarding industry
The last few years have seen rapid changes in the structure of the forwarding industry. The large companies have grown, mainly by acquiring their competitors. In the last two years, AEI, a large American-based forwarder, has bought Pandair to create AEI/Pandair. Similarly, the Rockwood Group has brought together Mercury Airfreight and Walford Meadows to form Rockwood International.

Yet, along with the few large companies, there are thousands of small freight forwarders. Many are clustered around airports, such as Heathrow, or ports like Dover, but they also exist in almost every commercial centre around the country. A small forwarder can build up a good business by serving local industry and by providing a far more personalised service than larger competitors. Between the large freight forwarders and the small ones stand the medium-sized companies which, as in other industries, are feeling the squeeze from both sides.

Freight forwarding is highly competitive and profit margins are not high. In addition, freight forwarders have a poor reputation among potential employees as salaries within the industry are generally low.

Entry to the industry is easy. Install a telephone, a fax machine and a typewriter, and anyone can call himself a freight forwarder. Unfortunately, there are too many of these 'fly-by-night' companies. Without financial resources, they struggle and often collapse only to re-emerge under another name a short while later. These forwarders besmirch the reputation of the whole industry and every shipper must be on guard against them.

British International Freight Association

The professional body for the freight forwarding industry is the British International Freight Association (BIFA). BIFA was created in 1989 and was formerly known as the Institute of Freight Forwarders (IFF). The IFF suffered from the fact that large numbers of freight forwarders chose not to join the organisation, and this weakened its claim to represent the industry. The change of name from IFF to BIFA marks a symbolic break with the past and a new beginning. The membership criteria of the BIFA are wider than those of the IFF, and membership is now open to many more types of business than before. In addition, the BIFA is making major efforts to attract more freight forwarding members and to offer a more attractive range of membership benefits.

The aim of the BIFA is to elevate the status of freight forwarders and to provide professional leadership in an important sector of industry.

Membership of the BIFA

Exporters and importers who select a freight forwarder should ensure that the company is a *registered trading member* of the BIFA rather than just a trading member which is a type of second-class membership. Freight forwarders who are registered trading members will generally display this fact on their letterhead and other documentation and will be pleased to use the achievement of this status in every aspect of their marketing.

The advantage of using a registered trading member of the BIFA is that the trader can be certain that the forwarder has fulfilled certain financial criteria and that their terms of trading have also been approved by the BIFA. The financial criteria mean that the forwarder should not in normal circumstances go into liquidation, although nothing can be guaranteed. Certainly, a financial crisis is less likely for a registered trading member than for one who does not belong to the BIFA. A freight forwarding company which collapses creates great problems for the customers who are left behind; frequently, goods are abandoned on some distant quay, storage charges mount rapidly, and freight usually has to be paid twice before the goods are released.

Members of the BIFA will use the Standard Trading Conditions (1989) which the BIFA itself has established. Standard Trading Conditions provide the legal framework for the relationship between forwarders and their customers. The conditions become important when problems arise and the BIFA conditions are supposed to be equitable to both sides. Many commentators reject this assertion and claim that some of the conditions will fall foul of the Unfair Contract Terms Act. The 1989 conditions are, however, still too new to have been put to a test in the courts. The BIFA conditions, despite their perceived weaknesses, do offer shippers far more safeguards than conditions adopted by many companies who do not belong to the BIFA; their failure to adopt the BIFA conditions is precisely the reason why they are not members. This is particularly the case with some of the courier and express companies which are generally not members of the BIFA and whose conditions can be far more restrictive than the BIFA ones.

Therefore, for reasons of greater financial security and the superior trading conditions, it is certainly better to use a freight forwarder who is a member of the BIFA.

Large or small forwarder

Smaller companies may be superficially attracted to smaller freight forwarders. Smaller firms have certain advantages – they usually provide a far more personalised service and every account is far more important to them than to a large firm. There is the possibility of establishing a personal relationship with the owner of the company. In addition, the smaller forwarder may have an office nearby – an added convenience.

Large freight forwarders have recognised many of the advantages provided by their smaller competitors, and large firms have opened small branch offices throughout the UK. The idea is to provide an individual service, although the customers benefit from the larger resources of the whole group.

A large freight forwarder is much more likely to operate its own service to most popular destinations in the world than a small company which will frequently pass freight on to another company. The larger company, thanks to its greater financial strength, will also provide far more options as well as a more thorough knowledge of specialised markets. Yet many of the larger companies cannot hope to offer a personalised service and this deters many shippers. In addition, because of relatively poor salaries, large firms have high staff turnover. This is particularly a problem in South East England, and the rapid change of staff leads to communication problems and the mishandlling of freight. Smaller companies tend to attract loyal staff, if only because the employees are better paid.

Horses for courses

Shippers who handle a few shipments a month should channel all their business through one freight forwarder. Once the volume of business reaches a creditable amount, it may be worth considering splitting the business between two freight forwarders. The normal reason for dividing business is to keep both suppliers on their toes. This may be the case, although it seems an unconvincing explanation.

The best reason for splitting business is because different freight forwarders specialise in different types of business. A forwarder, based at an airport, is likely to specialise in air freight rather than sea freight, so this may be one way of splitting up traffic. Other forwarders specialise in certain markets, so it may be worthwhile employing one specialist to handle freight to Africa and hand everything else to another firm.

Most freight forwarders will pretend that they can handle anything and they will certainly attempt to provide a universal service. Unfortunately, shippers need to look behind the veil of rhetoric and select forwarders who have an in-depth knowledge of particular markets or who provide specific services.

Conclusion

There are many good reasons for using a registered trading freight forwarder but, once that preliminary decision has been made, the particular company still needs to be selected. The precise choice, whether of a large, medium or small freight forwarder, depends on various factors which have been outlined. In addition to this detailed information, the best recommendation is still word of mouth. Ask fellow exporters and importers and contact the companies they mention. Look out for companies which carry British Standard 5750 registration (see page 164). In addition, consult some of the trade publications which carry advertisements and articles about the latest developments in international transport.

Chapter 12

Distribution, Marketing and Cash Flow

Introduction

The distribution function has not traditionally been given a high status in most companies. Most small companies have a financial director, accountant or bookkeeper to look after the finances of the firm, but how many have a distribution manager? Distribution is often regarded as an inevitable expense in much the same way as an electricity bill.

The rise in the price of oil in 1973 led to transport costs being scrutinised for the first time. From that time they were, of necessity, regarded by many companies as a significant expense. Suddenly, transport costs, whether for domestic or international distribution, rose sharply and had an impact on the profit and loss account and thus assumed much greater importance.

The perils of isolating transport costs

Many companies still look at their distribution costs in isolation and this often lead to attempts to reduce them. Hauliers or freight forwarders are accustomed to being summoned and told that transport costs must be reduced by a certain percentage. Sometimes the incumbents agree uneasily to the proposals, and on other occasions they will decide that the proposed rates are totally uneconomic and so reluctantly withdraw from servicing the account.

In the transport industry there are always some firms who manage to quote rates which most of their competitors call crazy; these firms often win business in these circumstances. Some companies can operate certain accounts more cheaply because of their own particular operational requirements, while other cheap operators are permanently walking the tightrope between solvency and liquidation.

An example of what can go wrong in the transport industry occurred in 1989 when Eagle Express went into liquidation with debts of around £35 million. The company used to operate an express delivery service throughout the UK and was probably surprised by the sheer speed at which trading losses accumulated. Many lesser known names disappear from the transport world every week – the main lesson for traders is to avoid dealings with such high-risk companies. To avoid handing goods over to such companies, certain precautions can be taken. Membership of the BIFA ensures a certain level of financial probity and integrity, and members are proud to display the BIFA logo on their letterhead and publicity material. In addition, exporters and importers can take the routine measure of asking for customer references.

Transport and marketing

The sensible way of looking at transport costs is to examine them in conjunction with other costs. This allows a company to make choices. The result of these choices is frequently to spend more money on transport in order to save far more substantial sums in other areas. Transport is not an isolated item of expenditure; it affects every other aspect of the business, and every transport decision taken should be examined in the light of its ramifications for the other parts of the business.

The easiest way to examine this link is to look at an example of a small UK exporter of giftware who had a steady stream of orders from small distributors in Singapore. Orders were received on a regular basis and, in most cases, the goods took between two to three weeks to manufacture. Once an order was ready, the goods were packed into cartons, and the exporter asked his freight forwarder to collect the consignment. The forwarder operated a regular consolidation service so, in most cases, the goods left on a vessel within about a week after collection from the giftware exporter. About four weeks later the goods were received by customers in Singapore.

On his annual visit to Singapore, the exporter asked several of his customers what he could do to persuade them to place more orders with him. The problem, according to the customers, was that the time lag from placing the order to delivery varied from as little as six weeks to as long as nine weeks. In either case urgent orders could not be directed to the UK supplier as even six weeks was an unacceptable delay.

On his return the exporter examined the possibility of sending his goods by air to Singapore. The cost was higher but the total order time could be reduced to between two and a half and three and a half weeks. The company then began to despatch everything by air and soon found that the volume of orders was increasing. Urgent orders, which could command a higher price, were being sent for the first time.

A few months later the exporter formalised these new arrangements by circulating a price list which stated 'all orders will be delivered within four weeks'. Later on the same company decided to expand its sales efforts to other parts of the region, and it now sends goods by air to a number of different countries, including the demanding Japanese market.

Examination, in isolation, of the cost of transport for this company would show a sharp increase from one year to the next as traffic switched from sea to air. The benefits appear at a later date as profits from sales which would never have been made under the previous arrangements. By the time the price list was printed, the company had made a definite decision to incorporate transport as an integral part of a planned marketing strategy.

Transport should always be regarded as part of a marketing strategy. This seems an obvious enough statement but many companies fail to link the two disciplines. A convincing sales presentation can persuade a customer to buy the product; if the goods turn up several weeks later, perhaps damaged as well, the sales presentation becomes the only memorable feature about the supplier. Yet many sales staff have to sell their company's products consistently against the background of poor transport arrangements – whether internationally or nationally.

The link between transport and marketing must, therefore, be made by every small company that can benefit substantially from providing its customers with a reliable delivery service. As the importance of transport as part of the marketing strategy is increasingly recognised, small companies can acquire a competitive advantage by promoting their delivery service against their larger competitors whose service may be slower and more bureaucratic.

The word often used to describe the science of transport is 'logistics', which combines all these elements – transport, storage and information systems – in an overall strategy. Like many words with a Greek derivation, logistics tends to confuse people, and there are so many different definitions that it would be unwise to add to the debate here. Almost inevitably, the science of logistics has spawned its own band of logistics consultants who will advise companies on the best way of organising their transport. Logistics consultants can be expensive, particularly if they come from large companies with heavy overheads. There are a small number of independent transport consultants who will undertake assignments which last a few days at a reasonable cost. In many cases outside advice, if required, can be obtained from a knowledgeable haulier or freight forwarder at no charge, although some business in return would be expected.

In fact, the decision on the most appropriate method of transport and the carrier can logically be evaluated from a brief study of the more important aspects listed here.

Type of goods

This will be a major consideration. Low-value goods are more likely to go by sea than by air as are heavier consignments. In addition, the size of the cargo may dictate the method of transport; diamonds, for example, always travel by air. Large pieces of equipment may not be appropriate for air freight as aircraft have size and weight limitations. Another important consideration is to maximise the capacity of the available unit. If a consignment bound for the Continent can use the full capacity of a 20′ container, this is preferable to half-filling a 12 metre tilt trailer.

Packing

Packing costs must be examined in conjunction with transport costs. A despatch by air or road requires less packing than a despatch by sea (see Chapter 10), so the higher freight charges may be outweighed by savings in packing costs. Even when sending goods by sea, on many routes there is still the choice between a containerised service and a conventional one. Conventional shipment requires a greater degree of packing. Some goods are, of course, quite unsuitable for containerisation, and this too will influence the choice of despatch.

Legal requirements

The transport of many products is governed by legal requirements, either national or international. There are tight regulations concerning the transport of hazardous goods (see Chapter 8). Some types of goods cannot be shipped by air under any circumstances while others are restricted to cargo flights only. Similarly, for cross-Channel traffic, trailers with hazardous goods are often only accepted on freight-only ships and the ferry companies impose a hazard surcharge.

Freight movements by road are also subject to numerous statutory controls which limit lorry weights and restrict drivers' hours. Weekend driving is restricted, particularly in Austria, France, Italy and Switzerland, so for these countries it is much more difficult to arrange the delivery of goods on a Monday morning. In such a situation, the trader may have to consider sending some of the freight by air or perhaps trying to persuade the customer to accept delivery on a Tuesday. Freight forwarders should always be in a position to advise their clients on how these restrictions hamper transport operations.

Location of consignor and consignee

The exact location of the consignor and consignee also influences the ultimate choice of transport. Many small high technology companies have established themselves around Heathrow Airport, London, so that the despatch and receipt of cargo can be more easily and quickly arranged than if they were situated in a remote part of the country. Similarly, a trader located near Felixstowe is more likely to be drawn to road transport to get goods across to the Continent.

It is also worthwhile looking at the position of the consignee in relation to the transport infrastructure of the country. Frequently, shippers send all their cargo for the USA to New York, mainly because this is the one place everyone has heard of. But it is not uncommon for the importer to be situated further away from New York than the UK supplier. In these circumstances it is far more sensible to route the goods via an American airport which is nearer to the importer, even if the goods require transhipment at some point during the journey.

Speed

It would not occur to anyone to send a heart pacemaker to the USA by sea. A box of bolts, however, is perhaps not so critical and can safely be sent by sea. Therefore, in many cases the type of cargo determines the speed of transport. High-value goods, such as medical equipment, computer parts and spare parts for machinery, tend to travel by air. Fresh fruit, vegetables and flowers must also be sent by air freight over longer distances, as they might otherwise arrive in unsaleable condition.

There are additional choices which can be made even within the same mode of transport. Shipping lines have different schedules depending on their ports of call and the actual speed of their ships, so companies deciding to send goods by sea must choose between the shipping lines on the basis of speed.

Transit time

The required transit time for the consignment will influence the method of transport. Clearly, if the shipment has to be in Australia within a week, air freight is the only option. Yet even within air freight, there is a choice to be made – direct booking with the airline or with a consolidation service which may only leave two or three times a week (see Chapter 4). Similarly, with road services to the Continent, the decision in principle must be followed up by a detailed analysis of the road options – express carrier or a groupage operator.

Frequency

Frequency of service is particularly important for small, high-value traffic. Many European motor car manufacturers produce different parts of the car in several countries. Absence of a single component can disrupt a production schedule and many manufacturers rely on a daily delivery service. For these companies the frequency of any transport service is critical. Many UK manufacturers who supply French and German car companies need a daily delivery. So a transport firm which promises two departures each week to Paris is automatically excluded, however quick the transit time.

Frequent services are now available for every method of transport. Ro-Ro ferries run across to the Continent every day except Christmas Day. Most major international centres are served by the airlines at least once a day – and often more frequently. Shipping lines on inter-continental routes also now offer regular departures, often as many as two sailings a week.

Reliability

Speed and frequency are of no value without reliability. For shippers this means that the services they use, whether by air, road or sea, should depart and arrive in accordance with the advertised schedule. The service must be equally reliable where documentation is concerned, as exporters and importers have to be certain of receiving the relevant documents from their nominated carriers in good order and as quickly as possible.

Terms of delivery

If goods are sold by a UK exporter on ex works or FOB terms (see Chapter 9), the transport decision has largely been abrogated in favour of the customer overseas who will normally dictate the method of transport and the carrier. In these circumstances much of this analysis becomes superfluous and the shipper has to follow the instructions of the consignee.

However, although ex works and FOB cargo becomes the consignee's responsibility, the nature of the sales contract can result in the exporter facing increased costs. If, under an FOB contract, the exporter located near Southampton is asked to use a vessel which calls at Liverpool, it is the exporter who has to pay for the increased costs of inland haulage. Ex works or FOB shipments remove the responsibility for the shipment from the exporter but this is a mixed blessing.

Letters of credit

Many goods exported overseas are sold against a letter of credit, opened by the importer. In these circumstances, reliability is critical. The terms of the letter of credit must be followed strictly, and the overseas customer will often impose conditions which are conclusive in deciding the method of transport. This can even happen where goods are sold on a c & f basis when the shipper should have the choice of method and carrier. Yet if the letter of credit nominates shipment via XYZ Line, the exporter can either comply or try to have the terms of the letter of credit changed by the importer.

If the letter of credit states 'shipment before 30 October', and the shipper chooses a line which sails on the following day, it is best either to select another line or to attempt to persuade the customer to amend the terms of the letter of credit. Another danger with letters of credit is the possibility of penalty clauses if the goods arrive late or import permits are only valid after a certain date. Commercially, however, a request for a change in the terms of the letter of credit can be a sensitive matter. The importer has to agree and initiate these changes, and many exporters will be reluctant to put their customers to additional trouble unless there are exceptional circumstances. Also, every amendment to a letter of credit will lead to a charge from the issuing bank, and this can again lead to unnecessary friction between the customer and the supplier.

Cash flow

One of the other major influences on the choice of the method of transport is cash flow. This factor has been recognised only by a small number of shippers in recent years, but it should be a major factor influencing every exporter and importer. Unfortunately, the division of responsibility, even within small firms, between transport and finance departments means that this key factor is often ignored.

The importance of cash flow arises from the fact that overseas importers normally do not pay for goods until after they have been delivered. Consider the following example. Goods sent by sea to the Far East will take about four weeks to reach their destination. If a customer has agreed to pay 30 days after the arrival of the goods, the UK supplier will be paid approximately two months after the goods have been despatched. If the same shipment is sent by air, the transit time is normally three to four days followed by the 30-day period. In this case, the UK supplier will receive payment within about five weeks, which is three weeks earlier than if the shipment had been sent by sea.

The three-week saving becomes particularly relevant for companies which finance their export sales by borrowing money from the banks. Interest rates tend to go up and down, but in recent years small firms have been forced to pay between 12 per cent and 18 per cent interest on overdrafts and borrowing facilities. The amount of interest paid has to be set against any additional freight sums incurred by sending the consignment by air instead of by sea.

In the example given, the exporter saves three weeks' bank interest if the goods are sent by air. The air freight charge will inevitably be higher than the sea freight cost and the exporter can compare the saving in bank interest charges against the additional freight payable. If the interest charges exceed the freight costs, it may be a good idea to send the consignment by air. If the additional freight charges are higher than the interest costs, shipment by sea must be favoured.

The terms of payment agreed between the buyer and seller are an important factor in the management of cash flow. They can vary but, in most cases, the exporter extends credit terms to his customer overseas.

148

Delays in payment can be quite short – seven days – but can also extend to three or six months. It is still quite rare for exporters to be paid while the goods are in transit and, for accountancy purposes, one must regard goods in transit as stock. The higher the stock level, the greater the drain on working capital, so quicker transit times will result in a better use of cash resources.

The effect of quicker transit times on cash flow can be extended and some companies reduce the number of their distributors and warehouses overseas. A company with strong sales in the USA may feel it necessary to hold some

Type of goods	AIR Needs less packing than sea despatch. Speedy.	SEA Needs more packing than air despatch. Speed of ship and ports of call vary between lines.	ROAD/SEA Consider packing; lorry weights; drivers' hours; weekend driving restrictions
Low value	–	✓	✓
High value	✓	–	–
Large	✓	✓	✓
Small	✓	–	–
Long-distance fruit, flowers and vegetables	✓	–	–
Hazardous restricted movement	Probably cargo flights only	Possibly freight only ships Surcharges on ferries	✓

Other considerations to be borne in mind for each consignment include:

- Location of consignor and consignee in relation to transport infrastructure
- Transit time
- Frequency of service
- Reliability of service
- Terms of delivery
- Payment terms
- Effect on cash flow of quick/slow delivery

Table 12.1 *Quick reference table for non-parcel despatches*

stocks over there. Such a decision is inevitable if sea freight is the chosen mode of transport – the transit time exceeds one week and US customers demand quick service. However, if the goods are sent by air, orders can reach their destination direct from the UK within five days. The costs of air freight will be higher but the exporter avoids the heavy costs of holding stocks overseas.

Transport Distribution Analysis

Another way of looking at the whole area of transport and marketing is through Transport Distribution Analysis which is a useful tool and easy to understand.

Transport Distribution Analysis (TDA) examines all the options which can be used to distribute goods, and the most appropriate method is then selected. TDA is used much more widely for international traffic than for domestic distribution, if only because the options and variations are much wider for exports and imports than for domestic traffic. TDA combines all the elements in the transport equation and can be helpful for companies who want to decide between the various alternatives. TDA can be applied to shipments destined for the Continent but it is more helpful for inter-continental destinations. The choice for traffic to other parts of Europe is either road trailer, container or air freight and the transit times differ by only a few days. The impact of interest rates is, therefore, bound to be far smaller than in the case of inter-continental traffic.

Packing
Normally goods sent by air require less packing than goods sent by sea.

Delivery to airport/port
These costs will vary more in accordance with the distance of the factory from the port or airport than with any other factor. The costs of sending a collection vehicle are identical whether the goods are despatched by sea or by air.

Handling
This refers to the charges incurred for loading goods – in this case into a container for sea shipment or into an airline container or on to a pallet.

Documentation
The costs of documentation vary so little between mode of transport that any difference can be dismissed as irrelevant.

Figure 12.1. *A worked example of Transport Distribution Analysis*

Consignment: 50 cartons of machine spare parts – gross weight 1000 kilos 3 cubic metres – value ex works £10,000. The goods are to be shipped to Hong Kong. The Hong Kong importer will pay for the goods 60 days from the date of delivery.

	Air transport £	Sea transport £
Value ex works	10,000	10,000
1. Packing	35	80
2. Delivery to airport/port	25	25
3. Handling	40	30
4. Documentation	20	20
5. Air freight/Sea freight	1,000	160
6. Import duty	N/A	N/A
7. Delivery from airport/port to consignee	30	30
8. Insurance	20	50
9. Total cost delivered Hong Kong	11,170	10,395
10. Interest costs @ 18% for 70 and 100 days (to nearest £)	386	513
11. Total cost incl. interest	11,556	10,908
12. Cost difference	648 (5.9%)	
13. Time difference	30 days	
14. Freight cost per kilo	1.56	0.91

Note: This example is intended as a basic guide to the technique and the figures are based on several assumptions. Nevertheless, the impact of the bank borrowing is apparent. An explanation of each category is given in the text.

Air freight/sea freight

In the example, the air freight charge has been calculated on the basis of £1 per 1000 kilos, so 1000 kilos will cost £1000. The sea freight rate has been calculated on the basis of a rate of US$80 per cubic metre; so 3 × US$80 ÷ 1.50 (exchange rate of US dollar to UK pound) = 160.

Import duty

As most goods enter Hong Kong without having to pay import duty, this item does not apply. Import duty is, however, often charged on the CIF value, so a higher freight charge will also increase the amount of duty payable.

Delivery from airport/port to consignee
As with the initial collection and delivery charge, the amount will not differ according to the mode of transport but rather with the distance between the airport of port and the consignee.

Insurance
Insurance premiums for sending goods by air are generally lower than for goods sent by sea. This is because of the longer transit time of sea transport and the greater danger of damage to which the goods are exposed. In this example, the insurance has been calculated at 0.2 per cent of the value for air transport and 0.5 per cent for sea transport. Not too much importance should be attached to the actual figures which will in any case be quite different for other destinations and types of cargo. Additional costs are also added when calculating insurance premiums – insurance brokers will advise on this area.

Total cost
In this example the cost differences are quite apparent and it is substantially cheaper to send the goods by sea than by air.

Interest costs
This is the element which should be included in every comparison of freight options. In this example shipment by air will result in payment 70 days from the date of despatch. By sea freight, the transaction will take 100 days. It has also been assumed that the total value of the goods and the cost of the freight have been borrowed.

Using a rate of interest of 18 per cent, the interest charges are £386 and £513 respectively – a difference of £127 which reflects the additional month's wait for payment should the goods go by sea.

Total cost including interest
This figure has more relevance than the pure costs of the goods and freight charges total. Once this figure is available other comparisons can be made.

Cost difference
In this example, the cheaper method is clear-cut – by sea. The company will save just under 6 per cent if the goods are sent by sea.

Time difference
Against this cost saving, the customer receives the goods 30 days earlier.

Freight cost per kilo
This last item summarises the differences which can be expressed as a rate per kilo. This figure is arrived at by dividing the total costs including interest by the weight of the consignment.

Conclusion
In this example the result is obvious. Sea freight is a far cheaper option, and even the higher interest charges incurred are insufficient to bridge the gap between the two methods of transport. If cost is the only consideration, the shipment should be sent by sea.

The role of Transport Distribution Analysis

TDA can play a useful role in helping shippers to reach a decision. It is a relatively simple analytical tool to use and, with experience, the calculations become quick and easy. However, like all theories, TDA should not be followed slavishly. In the example discussed TDA pointed to shipment by sea, but this is a cost-based decision only.

The distribution decision must be part of an overall marketing strategy, and this will often dictate a more expensive method of despatch to satisfy customers' requirements. Customer satisfaction is as important as the financial aspects, and companies should never be afraid to spend more money on distribution in order to meet customers' demands.

Distribution has an impact on every part of a small company's activities. It is important that every decision is taken in the light of its effect on the company's financial strength and marketing strategy. Viewed in isolation, it is easy for firms to take the wrong decisions, but linking distribution to the marketing strategy can have a positive effect on profitability – satisfied customers are likely to reorder and will also be more willing to pay slightly higher prices for a high-level service.

Chapter 13

Future Developments in International Transport

Introduction

Two current developments which will have a major impact on international distribution are the Single European Market (SEM) and the Channel Tunnel. They are often grouped together, mainly because they will take effect within a year of each other.

Another unconnected but important development is the growing concern in the transport industry with quality of service. One method for the independent verification of service level is the attainment of BS 5750 established by the British Standards Institute. It is applicable within the transport industry and many freight forwarders and hauliers are now in the process of applying for accreditation (see page 164).

The Single European Market

The SEM will begin on 1 January 1993. People refer to 1992 but this is one of those confusing shorthand expressions which has become part of everyday language and tends to confuse rather than illuminate. When people talk about 1992, they are usually referring to the creation of the SEM.

The SEM will not suddenly emerge on New Year's Day 1993 – it is intended to be the culmination of a long project begun several years ago. In addition, the SEM is a project which is intended for members of the European Community (EC) only, so any changes will affect trading arrangements with other members. It is possible that the EC will reach agreement with the members of the European Free Trade Association (EFTA) on certain matters but that has not yet happened. Companies which trade with other parts of the world – Africa, North America, the Far East – will not notice any changes in procedures. Trading conditions, of course, will continue to evolve.

Non-tariff barriers

The idea behind the creation of the SEM is the abolition of all barriers to trade within the EC. One of the original aims of the EC was the reduction

154

of tariff barriers among members. This has largely been achieved, and most goods move from one member state to another without the payment of customs duty.

Customs duties are, however, only one barrier to free trade and this realisation lies behind the impetus to create the SEM. For example, criteria for professional qualifications among member states are quite different; thus accountants, insurance brokers and other professionals cannot move easily between one country and another.

These barriers apply equally to international transport where each member state has its own regulations about drivers' hours, lorry weights, driving tests and many other items. By the time the SEM is created, the intention is for all non-tariff barriers to be standardised, so that a German haulier can operate as easily in the UK as he can in his own country. Equally, a British haulier will be able to operate in Munich as well as in Birmingham.

In addition to this attempt to standardise the legal framework which surrounds the transport industry, the SEM is trying to abolish much of the paperwork which surrounds intra-Community trade. So the ultimate aim is that it will be as easy to despatch goods from London to Milan as it is now to send them from London to Birmingham.

Many forecasters predict that the introduction of the SEM will act as a catalyst for small businesses and that small firms will be drawn into intra-EC trade for the first time. To a certain extent, this has already happened during the last few years, but even more small companies can be expected to begin to export and import once many of the barriers have been removed.

One misapprehension about the SEM is that all the planned changes will occur overnight on 31 December 1992. This is not the case; the creation of the SEM is a rolling programme of changes which will be introduced during the next few years. Many of the planned changes are of a technical nature, of interest principally to hauliers, freight forwarders and airlines. Exporters and importers do not require precise details of these proposals. Their potential effect is of more interest, although at the moment there is an element of speculation involved here. The major change which companies will notice concerns documentation.

Customs documentation within the EC

The principal document used for controlling intra-EC trade and monitoring trade statistics is the Single Administrative Document (SAD) (see Chapter 6). The SAD is a standard document which is now used by all EC member states as well as the EFTA countries. When the SAD was introduced in January 1988, it was intended as an interim stage on the road to the abolition of border controls for freight.

At the moment no final decision has been taken on which documents, if any, will be required after 1992. In theory, since no statutory documents are required when sending a parcel from Leeds to London, no paperwork should be needed when the goods move across from Germany to the UK. Traders and their suppliers will continue to produce whatever documents they require – invoices, packing lists, collection and delivery notes – but these are not a legal requirement. There are, however, problems still to be resolved by the member states and these relate to the requirement for trade statistics and VAT.

Trade statistics

The SAD is not only used by HM Customs to control the movement of goods to and from the UK, but also by the Department of Trade and Industry (DTI) to collect national trade statistics. This data supplies the balance of payment figures which the UK government publishes each month. If the SAD is abolished, some other method of collecting trade statistics will have to be found.

The DTI has not finalised its proposals, although one possible scheme is to ask exporters and importers to complete a return every month or perhaps less frequently. If this solution is adopted, it will impose an additional administrative burden on small companies which will eliminate any savings gained by the abolition of customs forms.

VAT

VAT is collected on imported goods. Some companies have a deferment (see Chapter 7), and this unique number is entered on the SAD form; other firms pay the VAT at the time of importation. This source of revenue is so essential for every government that no scheme will be acceptable which jeopardises these enormous amounts. The principle of charging VAT will not change but the administration of the tax for imports might. No firm decision has yet been taken.

Abolition of the SAD

The precise fate of the SAD is still not known, although there is pressure for its abolition. At the moment, traders are accustomed to paying their freight forwarders to complete these documents on their behalf. These ancillary charges are an important source of revenue for every freight forwarder. If the form is abolished, however, freight forwarders will be unable to charge these amounts for shipments between the UK and the rest of the EC.

There is, therefore, a potential saving in shipping costs for every exporter and importer, although these cost reductions are unlikely to be realised. Many freight forwarders, particularly groupage operators, subsidise their freight rates as they manage to squeeze an adequate profit from the clearance charges. The abolition of these charges will oblige forwarders to increase their freight rates to compensate for the loss of revenue.

Cabotage

At the moment UK road vehicles can only carry goods between the UK and another country. It is forbidden for a UK road haulier to collect a load in Italy and deliver it to West Germany, and equally for a German haulier to collect a load in Birmingham and deliver it to London. Such prohibited activities are known as cabotage.

It is the intention of the EC to legalise cabotage before 1992, so allowing non-residents to offer road haulage and other transport services within a member state. The legalisation of cabotage will break down barriers which restrict national markets to domestic hauliers.

The reason for permitting cabotage is to try to fill some of the thousands of lorries which travel through Europe empty – prevented from looking for a return load by the existing cabotage rules. One recent study, by the accountancy firm Ernst and Whinney (now Ernst and Young), estimated the cost of empty running within the EC at about £830 million per year. Of this, 20 per cent was attributed to the existence of the cabotage restrictions. In an increasingly energy-conscious world, the prospect of large savings on fuel costs is a further incentive for EC governments to legalise cabotage.

There are, however, formidable obstacles to overcome before domestic haulage markets are opened up to free competition. Some domestic markets, particularly France and Germany, are more protected than the UK market, and these countries are more reluctant to open up their domestic markets than Britain.

In theory, UK traders should benefit from the abolition of cabotage, as greater competition might lead to a fall in haulage rates. Most road transport (up to 95 per cent) is domestic business, so the abolition of cabotage will open up an enormous new market. Yet even the abolition of cabotage will not lead to a totally free market – different rates of VAT and variations in fiscal regimes will make it difficult for a UK haulier to ply for domestic business on the Continent. There may be a slight reduction in rates, but it is unlikely to be of any great significance to the small trader – perhaps 1 or 2 per cent at the most. In addition, grave doubts still exist about whether unrestricted cabotage will be introduced by 1992.

Permits

The current regulations on cabotage are enforced by the permit rules which govern the numbers of trailers allowed to cross international borders. At the moment, the governments of the EC reach a bilateral arrangement every year to issue a certain number of permits. Each permit represents one journey or permission to cross frontiers for a period of time – perhaps a month or even a year. The permit total agreed, for example, by the UK and French governments is then divided into two and the Department of Transport in the UK and its French counterpart each issue the permits to their hauliers. In addition, the EC issues a certain number of permits which supplements the total.

The permit system used to act as a barrier to growth in the market; if a haulier was not in possession of a permit, he was prevented from accepting international traffic. Over recent years, the number of permits on issue has been increased substantially in order to end the shortage which only benefited fraudsters. As the number of permits has increased, the shortage has disappeared.

The stated policy of the EC is to continue to raise the number of permits every year, so eventually the numbers available will make the whole system superfluous. The Benelux countries have been operating without permits for several years. Small shippers do not have to worry themselves about the intricacies of the permit system, but it helps to be aware of its existence and the possibility of its abolition.

Vehicle weights

The EC has agreed on a standard weight limit of 40 tonnes which should apply in all the member states (see Chapter 3). The UK has obtained a derogation which postpones the requirement to raise the existing 38 tonne limit until 1999.

Once this new limit comes into force, many of the newer trailers will be able to accept higher payloads. This change is unlikely to have any noticeable effect on small companies – not many small firms have a shipment of 24 or 26 tonnes ready at the same time. Companies which do ship heavy cargo may benefit slightly from more goods being loaded on to the trailer and the costs per tonne falling. But 1999 is still a long way ahead.

Channel Tunnel

The Channel Tunnel is one of the largest and most ambitious transport projects attempted this century. Like all major undertakings, it has its quota of critics who are particularly vociferous whenever the project faces unexpected difficulties.

The Channel Tunnel will run from just outside Folkestone to Conquelles which is near Calais on the French coast. The length of the actual tunnel will be just over 50 kilometres (about 31 miles). The anticipated date for completion of the project is June 1993, and in November 1989 the estimated total cost was £7.5 billion. The costs have risen substantially since building began, and it is possible that £7.5 billion may not in the end be sufficient. There is also the possibility that the project will be abandoned, but this is becoming more and more unlikely with each passing month.

The owners of the tunnel are Eurotunnel, a publicly quoted company with a board of British and French directors. The contract for the construction of the tunnel has been awarded to Transmanche Link, a consortium of British and French construction companies. The project is being financed privately through bank loans and an issue of shares. Many commentators believe that at some stage the financial situation will become so grave that the British and French governments will have to lend Eurotunnel money to finish the project. Yet on the assumption that the Tunnel will be completed, it will provide traders on both sides of the Channel with a whole range of new transport options.

Transport through the Tunnel

The Tunnel will be a rail tunnel only and all freight passing through it will be on trains. Three tunnels are being built – one in each direction and a service tunnel in the middle. It is important to realise that, although British Rail (BR) and their French counterparts Société Nationale des Chemins de Fer Francais (SNCF) will be important users of the Tunnel, they are not the owners. BR and SNCF have already made contractual arrangements with Eurotunnel to use a certain amount of the Tunnel capacity.

Shippers, therefore, will have two ways in which they can use the Tunnel: either as a cross-Channel link only or using the services of the railway authorities who will provide a through service linking many UK towns with commercial centres on the Continent.

Folkestone/Calais link

Eurotunnel is building two large terminals for both passengers and freight at either end of the Tunnel. Once the Tunnel is open, lorries will be able to arrive at the Folkestone terminal and drive on to a shuttle train. Freight trains will be separate from passenger ones but will depart frequently throughout the day and night. Once in Calais, the driver will take his vehicle off the train and continue on his way. This shuttle operation will compete directly with the existing ferry routes.

159

The type of operation envisaged is ideal for driver-accompanied trailers (see Chapter 3) but unaccompanied traffic poses an operational problem. Once Eurotunnel has to start loading and unloading trailers, valuable time is lost at either end of the journey, and the Tunnel concept is being sold to international hauliers on the basis that time can be saved by using the Tunnel. There are also unresolved problems regarding the transport of hazardous cargo through the Tunnel about which no final decisions have yet been taken.

Rail options

The opening of the Channel Tunnel will present both BR and SNCF, and to a lesser extent other European railways, with a unique opportunity to provide a whole range of new services. About 2 per cent of the UK's international trade is currently moved by rail, but the number of types of goods appropriate for rail transport is very restricted (see Chapter 3) and rail freight has not been a viable option for small traders for many years.

BR's intention is to increase its market share significantly and, to its credit, BR has realised that the Channel Tunnel is a once-in-a-century opportunity to make up some of the ground lost during the past 20 years. The problem facing BR is credibility in the market-place – BR does not have a particularly favourable public image. Yet as a freight carrier, BR has made progress during the past few years. It has introduced an excellent computer system which monitors the position of every wagon, and transit times and service levels have improved. The chief disadvantage of sending goods by rail is the danger of strikes. Just as BR was rebuilding its reputation, a series of strikes during the summer of 1989 cast doubt once more on its reliability in the freight industry.

The aim of Railfreight Distribution is to capture a 30 per cent market share of all journeys to or from the UK whose distance exceeds 300 kilometres (187 miles). Cargo can be shipped via Railfreight Distribution using several options. The Channel Tunnel will allow hauliers and freight forwarders to offer transport using both road and rail. This can be done by using swap bodies or containers.

Swap bodies

The swap body is a vehicle which can be transferred between road and rail. The opening of the Channel Tunnel will ensure the wider acceptance of this vehicle in the UK. A swap body (see Figure 13.1) in many ways resembles a standard 12 metre tilt trailer. A swap body trailer arrives by road at a factory, collects the goods and then proceeds to the nearest railhead. Here the trailer will be lifted by a crane on to a rail wagon. Railfreight Distribution will then organise the movement of the wagon through the

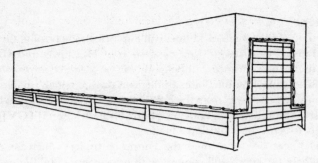

Figure 13.1 A swap body

Tunnel to its destination where the trailer will be lifted off the rail wagon and delivered by road to the consignee.

Swap body traffic has grown rapidly on the Continent where the number of trailers carried in this way has quadrupled in ten years. Swap bodies are not stacked but, as most of their journey is by rail, the weight restrictions are higher. In theory, swap bodies can weigh up to 44 tonnes under load, although allowance must be made for the weight of the swap body and tractor. This will restrict the carrying capacity for cargo to about 26–28 tonnes, but this is a much higher weight limit than will ever be carried on a door-to-door road movement.

Containers

Railfreight Distribution anticipates that container transport to the Continent will undergo a further revival once the Tunnel is complete. Railfreight Distribution operates its own Freightliner containers, but will also handle containers belonging to other companies. With the Channel link, there will be a faster transit time, and container operators will be able to use the rail system instead of the ferry services.

The containers used will be no different from the containers currently in use, except that the range of units available may broaden. The existence of the Tunnel is expected to lead to an increase in demand for containers, perhaps at the expense of trailers.

Rail wagons

For companies with a large quantity of goods to move, there is already the possibility of using a dedicated wagon to carry the goods (see Chapter 3). The Tunnel will certainly speed up transit times, but the movement of full rail wagons will still remain of primary interest to companies which have a large amount of freight to move at one time.

Air freight

The opening of the Channel Tunnel will also bring new possibilities for air freight traffic. With the growing congestion of Heathrow and Gatwick, airports in northern France and Belgium will be able to compete with the UK airports. Lille/Lesquin, for example, is at the moment a small regional airport only an hour away from the French coast. The intention is to link the airport to the new high-speed rail line (Train Grande Vitesse [TGV]) which will run between Calais and Paris via Lille.

Air freight can be sent through the Tunnel on trailers which can then go to Lille where the goods will connect with inter-continental flights. There are already direct flights from Lille/Lesquin to New York, and the opening of the Tunnel may lead to more inter-continental flights landing at Lille to serve the UK market as well as neighbouring Belgium and France itself.

Unlike Heathrow and Gatwick, Lille/Lesquin has enormous capacity to handle more flights and can also provide rapid ground handling. The total journey time, using the Tunnel, will not exceed the current transit time using the congested airports in South East England.

Method of operation

Once the Tunnel is open, Railfreight Distribution intends to operate 27 trains per day in each direction. This number will increase as more traffic is attracted to the Tunnel alternative. Containers, swap bodies and rail wagons will all go forward on the same service.

Railfreight Distribution intends to introduce a timetabled service which will link UK regional centres with major towns on the Continent. The transit times already advertised are impressive – Birmingham to Paris or Brussels will take 18 hours, Birmingham to Basle, Bordeaux, Cologne and Lyons 24 hours, Birmingham to Madrid, Milan and Turin 36 hours and Birmingham to Vienna 42 hours. These train services will be attractive to hauliers and freight forwarders. There are already indications of UK firms investing in swap bodies rather than in standard tilt trailers so that they can avail themselves of the new opportunities presented by the Tunnel.

Channel Tunnel v Ro-Ro ferries

Before the Tunnel was commissioned, ferry operators mounted a vociferous campaign against the project. Their aim was to stop the Tunnel – but they failed. Nevertheless, the long lead time required to build the Tunnel has given the ferry companies several years in which to prepare for the Tunnel and mount a competitive challenge. The ferry operators are investing in new, larger ships and taking other initiatives which will allow them to provide competition with the Tunnel.

One area of keen competition will be price. Eurotunnel is still being very coy about the charges to carry a road vehicle through the Tunnel. This reluctance arises from the fact that they are not yet certain what the final building costs will be. The ferry companies may try to maintain their market share by a price war which they can probably withstand more easily than Eurotunnel, which will want to recoup some of the £7 billion invested in the project.

Another area of competition for the two modes of transport will be speed. Using the Tunnel will undoubtedly be quicker than using the ferry but for freight the time saving will not be significant. For example, a trailer which leaves London on Monday afternoon has to be in Paris on Tuesday morning. This can easily be achieved by using the ferry, and the crossing provides an opportunity for the driver to relax and spend some time with other drivers. The Tunnel will perhaps get the vehicle to Calais a little earlier, but the driver will travel alone and remain throughout the journey in his cab. The Tunnel route may well enable the load to reach Paris by 4 or 5am, but this will not be all that helpful as businesses open at 8am.

The effect of the Tunnel on small businesses

Although small exporters and importers will not become involved directly in organising the movement of goods through the Tunnel, the details are important as transport links to the Continent will change dramatically. Forwarders and road hauliers need to have an intricate knowledge of how the Tunnel will operate, and they will choose whether customers' goods should be shipped by ferry or through the Tunnel.

Traders should, however, be aware of the new options which the Tunnel will present. Groupage shipments (see Chapter 3) could be loaded into a swap body and sent by rail to a depot on the Continent for onward delivery by road to their destination. Freight forwarders may also begin to load groupage cargo destined for the Continent into containers. The competition between the Tunnel and the ferries may lead to a price war which could lower the rates on offer to traders. The old rivalry between road and rail will weaken as the two modes of transport have the opportunity to become mutually dependent.

Companies which have trading links with other parts of the world will also have more options for their freight once the Tunnel is open. Containers from the Far East may be unloaded at a Continental port, such as Antwerp or Le Havre, and then sent through the Tunnel on block trains to the UK. This may be more economical for some shipping lines than the option of sending the vessel to call at a UK port or of organising a small feeder ship to bring the UK bound cargo across the Channel.

The most directly affected ferry routes are those based on the south coast – Dover, Folkestone and Ramsgate. Services which operate across the

Western Channel, from Poole or Portsmouth, and across the North Sea, from Felixstowe or Hull, are further away and less vulnerable to competition from the Tunnel.

British Standard 5750

The British Standards Institute (BSI) has issued guidelines on the quality of its products for many years. The BSI monogram, which is a small kitemark, can be seen on all types of goods. The BSI mark is not, however, a guarantee – the Titanic was made to a BSI standard!

One of the more recent British Standards is number 5750 which can be applied to service operations – international hauliers and freight forwarders. This is a quality assurance management system, and successful companies have the right to use a special logo. The award of the BS 5750 registration is an assurance to customers that the quality of a company's services is of a proven standard. To achieve the valuable BS 5750 approval, the applicant has to examine all its procedures and then open its doors to BSI inspectors who will assess every aspect of the operation in relation to the standard.

The length of time taken to acquire approval depends on how far an individual company has gone towards documenting its control procedures. A few transport firms have already achieved BS 5750 recognition, but they are still a small minority. Many more companies are in the process of applying, and the number of firms who will be granted BS 5750 will increase substantially during the next few years.

For small exporters and importers, BS 5750 indicates adherence to disciplined procedural quality control and there is a strong case for enquiring whether a freight forwarder or haulier has achieved the BS 5750 registration. An affirmative answer means that the company is dedicated to providing a quality service and has been willing to expose its operational procedural control to BSI assessment. BS 5750 means that systems exist for handling cargo and for instigating appropriate corrective action techniques for any problems which might arise.

Companies which achieve BS 5750 will be delighted to advertise their success by use of the registered firm logo. As the standard is open equally to small, medium and large transport firms, it is worthwhile favouring a BS 5750 company over a non-participant in the scheme because that company has demonstrated its commitment to quality. The overall objective of BS 5750 is to raise the standard of the transport sector, and it is an initiative worthy of support from small exporters and importers.

The international equivalents of BS 5750 are ISO 9000 and EN 29000.

Conclusion

Apart from the changes to distribution which will result from the creation of the SEM, the Channel Tunnel and BS 5750, small traders have to keep abreast of developments in data processing, principally EDI (see Chapter 6).

Many commentators have observed that the patterns and options in distribution are set to change very rapidly during the next ten years. These changes, many of which cannot be predicted at the moment, provide both an opportunity and a threat. Many small companies will be able to harness these changes to create a competitive advantage for their businesses, while others may remain tied to outdated methods of distribution. Every small business faces the challenge of reviewing its distribution arrangements at regular intervals and changing them in the light of developments in the field of transport. The analysis and decision-making are not easy but they are essential for small companies which want to grow and thrive into the next century.

Principal Ro-Ro Ferry Services between the UK/Continent, Eire and Scandinavia

UK port	Continental port	Country	Operator
Chatham	Hamburg	W. Germany	Bore Line
Chatham	Helsinki	Finland	Bore Line
Chatham	Zeebrugge	Belgium	Kent Line
Dartford	Zeebrugge	Belgium	Kent Line
Dover	Boulogne	France	P & O European Ferries
Dover	Calais	France	P & O European Ferries
Dover	Calais	France	Sealink British Ferries
Dover	Dunkirk	France	Sealink British Ferries
Dover	Ostend	Belgium	P & O European Ferries
Dover	Zeebrugge	Belgium	P & O European Ferries
Felixstowe	Europoort	Netherlands	P & O European Ferries
Felixstowe	Göteborg	Sweden	DFDS
Felixstowe	Helsinki	Finland	Finanglia Ferries
Felixstowe	Oslo	Norway	Fred Olsen Lines
Felixstowe	Rotterdam	Netherlands	DFDS
Felixstowe	Zeebrugge	Belgium	P & O European Ferries
Fishguard	Rosslare	Eire	Sealink British Ferries
Folkestone	Boulogne	France	Sealink British Ferries

UK port	Continental port	Country	Operator
Grangemouth	Hamburg	W. Germany	Washbay Line
Great Yarmouth	Scheveningen	Netherlands	Norfolk Line
Great Yarmouth	Esbjerg	Denmark	Britline
Grimsby	Esbjerg	Denmark	DFDS
Grimsby	Esbjerg	Denmark	Millau Line
Harwich	Antwerp	Belgium	Cobelfret
Harwich	Bremerhaven	W. Germany	DFDS
Harwich	Bremerhaven	W. Germany	Argo Line
Harwich	Bremerhaven	W. Germany	Bore Line
Harwich	Cuxhaven	W. Germany	Bore Line
Harwich	Esbjerg	Denmark	DFDS
Harwich	Göteborg	Sweden	DFDS
Harwich	Hamburg	W. Germany	DFDS
Harwich	Helsingborg	Sweden	DFDS
Harwich	Hook of Holland	Netherlands	Sealink British Ferries
Harwich	Oslo	Norway	Fred Olsen Lines
Harwich	Oslo	Norway	DFDS
Harwich	Turku	Finland	Bore Line
Holyhead	Dublin	Eire	B & I Line
Holyhead	Dun Laoghaire	Eire	Sealink British Ferries
Hull	Europoort	Netherlands	North Sea Ferries
Hull	Rostock	E. Germany	DSR-Lines
Hull	Zeebrugge	Belgium	North Sea Ferries
Immingham	Cuxhaven	W. Germany	Elbe-Humber Roline
Immingham	Eemshaven	Netherlands	Euroliner
Immingham	Göteborg	Sweden	DFDS
Immingham	Hamburg	W. Germany	Elmskip
Immingham	Helsingborg	Sweden	DFDS
Immingham	Oslo	Norway	Fred Olsen Lines
Immingham	Rotterdam	Netherlands	DFDS
Immingham	Zeebrugge	Belgium	Cobelfret
Ipswich	Europoort	Netherlands	North Sea Ferries
Kings Lynn	Hamburg	W. Germany	Washbay Line

DISTRIBUTION FOR THE SMALL BUSINESS

UK port	Continental port	Country	Operator
Liverpool	Dublin	Eire	B & I Line
Liverpool	Dublin	Eire	Pandoro
Middlesbrough	Gdynia	Poland	Polish Ocean Lines
Middlesbrough	Göteborg	Sweden	Ferrymasters
Middlesbrough	Helsingborg	Sweden	Ferrymasters
Newhaven	Dieppe	France	Sealink Dieppe Ferries
Newhaven	Dieppe	France	Dieppe Ro-Ro
North Shields	Esbjerg	Denmark	DFDS
Pembroke	Rosslare	Eire	B & I Line
Poole	Cherbourg	France	Truckline
Portsmouth	Caen	France	Britanny Ferries
Portsmouth	Cherbourg	France	P & O European Ferries
Portsmouth	Cherbourg	France	Sealink British Ferries
Portsmouth	Le Havre	France	P & O European Ferries
Portsmouth	St Malo	France	Britanny Ferries
Purfleet	Gdynia	Poland	Polish Ocean Lines
Purfleet	Kotka	Finland	Finanglia Ferries
Purfleet	Helsinki	Finland	Finanglia Ferries
Purfleet	Rostock	E. Germany	DSR-Lines
Purfleet	Rotterdam	Netherlands	Finanglia Ferries
Plymouth	Roscoff	France	Brittany Ferries
Plymouth	Santander	Spain	Brittany Ferries
Ramsgate	Dunkirk	France	Sally Line
Ramsgate	Ostend	Belgium	Schiaffino Freight Ferries
Sheerness	Vlissingen	Netherlands	Olau Line
Swansea	Cork	Eire	Swansea Cork Ferries

UK port	Continental port	Country	Operator
Southampton	La Coruña (Corunna)	Spain	Vasco Line
Southampton	Lisbon	Portugal	Vasco Line
Teesport	Zeebrugge	Belgium	North Sea Ferries
Weymouth	Cherbourg	France	Sealink British Ferries

Göteborg is probably better known in English as Gothenburg, but the former name usually appears in atlases. Europoort used to be better known as Rotterdam.

Publications with Information on the Freight Industry

Air Cargo News International
Headline House
Chaucer Road
Ashford
Middlesex TW15 2QT
Tel: 0784 255000

British Shipper and Forwarder
Grenville House
7 Church Road
Teddington
Middlesex TW11 8PF
Tel: 081-977 9284

Export Digest
Croner House
London Road
Kingston upon Thames
Surrey KT2 6SR
Tel: 081-547 2776

Export Today
Europa House
13–17 Ironmonger Row
London EC1V 3QN
Tel: 071-253 2545

Freight News Express
35–39 Castle Street
High Wycombe
Buckinghamshire HP13 6RN
Tel: 0494 464 448

Handy Shipping Guide
230–234 Long Lane
London SE1 4QE
Tel: 071-403 4353

Importing Today
Europa House
13–17 Ironmonger Row
London EC1V 3QN
Tel: 071-253 2545

International Freighting Weekly
Maclean Hunter House
Chalk Lane
Cockfosters Road
Barnet
Hertfordshire EN4 0BU
Tel: 081-975 9759

Lloyd's Loading List
PO Box 111
Sheepen Place
Colchester CO3 3LP
Tel: 0206 772277

Motor Transport
Quadrant House
The Quadrant
Sutton
Surrey SM2 5AS
Tel: 081-661 3284

Transport Week
Morgan Grampian plc
40 Beresford Street
London SE18 6BR
Tel: 081-855 7777

World Freight
INC Publications
38 St John Street
London EC1M 4AY
Tel: 071-251 8798

Appendix 3
Glossary

ACP 90 computer system for customs clearance used at major UK airports
ADR Accord Dangereux Routier
ATA Carnet document accompanying exhibition goods
AWB air waybill

BAF bunker adjustment factor
Belly cargo hold of an aircraft
BIFA British International Freight Association
B/L bill of lading
BOTB British Overseas Trade Board
Box trailer trailer with solid sides
Boxes containers
BR British Rail
Break bulk non-containerised transport

CAA Civil Aviation Authority
CAF currency adjustment factor
CBI Confederation of British Industry
CFR cost and freight
CHIEF Customs Handing of Import and Export Freight
CIF cost, insurance and freight
CIP freight, carriage and insurance paid
Combi freight and passengers share the cabin of the aircraft
Conference group of shipping lines
Congestion surcharge surcharge imposed when ships are delayed in port
Consol consolidation
Consortium group of shipping lines providing a joint service
CRP Conveyance, Packaging and Labelling Regulations

DAF delivered to frontier
Datapost premium service of Royal Mail Parcels
DCP freight carriage paid
DDP delivery duty paid
DEPS Departmental Entry Processing System

Draw-bar trailer trailer in two parts
DTI Department of Trade and Industry; Direct Trader Input

EC European Community
EDI Electronic Data Interchange
EDIFACT international EDI standard
EFTA European Free Trade Association
Ex works all freight charges paid by the consignee
Excess claims up to a certain amount which will not be met
EXQ ex quay
EXS ex ship

FAK freight all kind
FAS free alongside ship
Fast lane system used for speeding up the customs clearance of EC goods
FCL full container load
FEFC Far East Freight Conference
FIATA International Federation of Freight Forwarders Association
Flat rack container for the transport of large pieces
Flat trailer trailer without a tilt
FLIC Forwarders' Local Import Clearance
FOA FOB airport
FOB free on board
FOR free on rail
40' container 40 foot in length
FOT free on truck
FRC free carrier
Freighter freight only aircraft
Freightliner container division of Railfreight Distribution
Full load trailer dedicated to one consignment only

GATT General Agreement on Tariffs and Trade
Groupage consolidation of smaller shipments into one load

Hague Visby Rules rules governing sea transport
HAWB house air waybill
Hire and reward hauliers carrying goods on behalf of other companies
HS Harmonised System

IATA International Air Transport Association
ICAO International Civil Aviation Organisation
ICC International Chamber of Commerce

IMCO International Maritime Consultative Organisation
IMDG Code International Maritime Dangerous Goods Code

LCL less than container load
LIC local import clearance
Low loader trailer for the transport of heavy loads

MAWB master air waybill

NFC National Freight Corporation
NIC newly industrialised country
NVOCC non-vessel owning common carrier

Open cover insurance covering multi-consignments over a period of time
Open top containers without a top
Outsider non-conference shipping line
Own account companies using their own vehicles for transport

Part load Substantial proportion of the trailer occupied by one consignment
PGR Road Traffic (Carriage of Dangerous Substances in Packages)

Railfreight Distribution Freight division of British Rail
Red Star Parcels Parcels service of British Rail
Removable roof containers with a removable roof
RHA Road Haulage Association
RMP Royal Mail Parcels
Ro-Ro roll-on, roll-off

SAD Single Administrative Document
SDR special drawing right
SEM Single European Market
Single voyage policy insurance valid for one journey
SITPRO Simplification of International Trade Procedures Board
Skeletal vehicle for carrying containers
Slot allocation method of allocating containers between shipping lines
SNCB Belgian Railways
SNCF French Railways
Stripped unloaded
Super cube trailer for the carriage of bulky goods
Swap body vehicle capable of travelling by road and rail

TDA transport distribution analysis
TDG Transport Development Group
Tilt trailer covered trailer
20′ container 20 foot long

ULD unit load device

VAT value added tax

W/M weight/measure
War risk surcharge imposed to meet the risk of war damage
Warsaw Convention rules governing air transport

Further Reading

Published by Kogan Page

Export for the Small Business (2nd edition), Henry Deschampsneufs (1988)
Importing for the Small Business (2nd edition), Mag Morris (1988)
A Manager's Guide to International Road Freighting, Largent Brown (1987)
   A list of books for small businesses is available from the publishers
The Transport and Distribution Manager's Guide to 1992, David Lowe (1989)
The Transport Manager's and Operator's Handbook 1990 (20th edition), David Lowe (1989)

Other books

Elements of Export Practice (2nd edition), Alan Branch, Chapman and Hall (1985)
Exporter and Forwarder: The Professional Guide 1990, British International Freight Association
Export Trade: Law and Practice of International Trade, Clive M Schmitthoff, Stevens & Sons (1986)
ICC Guide to Incoterms, International Chamber of Commerce (1990)
Report on the Market for Express Goods Services between the UK and Europe, North America, and the Far East, Institute of Logistics and Distribution Management (1989)

Index

A reference in italics indicates a figure or table.

accompanied trailers 31–2
Accord Dangereux Routier (ADR) 101
ACE consortium 62
'ACP 90' 93
ADR (Accord Dangereux Routier) 101
AEI/Pandair 138
agents, freight forwarder's role 132–3
air charters 49
air freight 14, 28–31, 43–52
  Channel Tunnel effects 162
  consolidation 50–51
  dangerous goods 100
  rates 49–50
  sea compared 44–5, 144–53, *149*, *151*
  transit time 45–6, 104
air freight wholesalers 50
air/sea freight 51–2
air waybills (AWBs) 70, 82–5, *83*, *84*, 131
Anglo Airlines 48
antiques/fine arts, transporting 97–8
Arab-British Chamber of Commerce 69
ATA carnets, 104, *105*
axle weights 36–7, 158
AWB *see* air waybills

BAF (bunker adjustment factor) surcharges 61
bags 123
barrels 124
BIFA *see* British International Freight Association
bills of lading (B/L) 70, 73–82, 91
  FIATA 78–81, *79*, *80*
  freight forwarder's 73, 81
  liner (ocean) *74*, *75*, 78
B/L *see* bills of lading
Boeing 747s 46, 47
Boeing 767s 28
bonded warehouses 135–6
books, transporting 98
box trailers, 34, *34*
'boxes' *see* containers
boxes (packaging) 123
British Airways, Singapore cargo 48
British International Freight Association (BIFA) *formerly* Institute of Freight Forwarders 143
  bills of lading 78
  EDI network 89
  registered membership 131, 139
  Standard Trading Conditions 131, 140
British Overseas Trade Board 103
British Rail (BR), Channel Tunnel 41, 159, 160–62
British Standard '5750' 138, 141, 164

177